THE LITTLE RED BOOK OF
HUNTER'S WISDOM

THE LITTLE RED BOOK OF
HUNTER'S WISDOM

Jay Cassell and Peter Fiduccia

Skyhorse Publishing

Skyhorse Publishing books may be purchased in bulk at special
discounts for sales promotion, corporate gifts, fund-raising, or
educational purposes. Special editions can also be created to
specifications. For details, contact the Special Sales Department,
Skyhorse Publishing, 307 West 36th Street, 11th Floor, New
York, NY 10018 or info@skyhorsepublishing.com.

Skyhorse® and Skyhorse Publishing® are registered trademarks of
Skyhorse Publishing, Inc.®, a Delaware corporation.

www.skyhorsepublishing.com

10 9 8 7 6 5 4 3 2 1

Library of Congress Cataloging-in-Publication Data is available
on file.
ISBN: 978-1-61608-393-9

Printed in China

Photo Credits:

Ted Rose: 9, 19, 26, 30, 33, 35, 36, 43, 44, 49, 52-53, 61, 66, 83,
    84, 89, 93, 127, 128, 136
Jay Cassell: vi, 39, 180-181
Peter Fiduccia: 2, 12, 113, 114, 119, 122
Shutterstock: 70, 73, 74, 77, 100, 103, 105, 106, 110

Contents

• Jay Cassell with Osceola gobbler, Lakeland, Florida.

Introduction

The Little Red Book of Hunter's Wisdom is a compilation of thought-provoking quotes about hunting—some old, some recent, some by well-known people, some by everyday folks. Our intention is that, if you take them as a whole, they will give you an overview of what this great sport of hunting is all about.

Peter and I assembled these quotes—all 363 of them—from a myriad of sources: my personal library, Peter's library, public libraries, websites, books lent to us by friends, the list goes on and on. When all is said and done, doing the research for this book was as much fun as actually assembling it. While the majority of the quotes are from books that Peter and I have read and remembered, many were taken from books that we researched—books that we knew about, but never had the chance to read. I knew, for example, that the Russian writer Ivan Turgenev had written about hunting in the nineteenth century; yet I had never read his "Sportsman's Notebook" before. What a fine piece of literature, what remarkable powers of observation. I returned that book to my local library, in South Salem, New York, and made a mental note to borrow it again.

There are other books I plan to revisit, some that I read more than 25 years ago, some I've never read. What a pleasure it was to once again read "The Leatherstocking Tales," by James Fenimore Cooper, which I hadn't looked at since high school. What joy I felt to open Hemingway's "Green Hills of Arica," another book I hadn't read in years.

Others I have read recently. Rudyard Kipling's "The Jungle Books" have always been among my favorites: My father read them to me when I was a boy, and I did the same with my children. I continue to pick up the two volumes and read them from time to time. It's always inspiring to read about the boy Mowgli, growing up with wolves; and the mongoose, Rikki-tikki-tavi, living with a human family and protecting them from Nag and Nagaina, the sinister cobras that inhabit the garden.

Some of the quotes in this book are from my mental library—passages I have read and remembered over the years, from stories I have enjoyed and related to. "Lost," by Burton Spiller, always struck a chord with me. What hunter hasn't considered the consequences of getting lost deep in the woods, with daylight fading?" The story took on special meaning to me when I became seriously turned around while deer hunting in Maine's Allagash region in the late 1980s: The temperature was near zero, the sun had dropped behind Mount Katahdin, and I was lost. Like Spiller, I made mistakes—in my case, I didn't trust my compass, and I set off in momentary panic, when I should have simply stopped and taken some time to calm down and think things through. Ultimately I did stop, and was able to figure out how to get back to camp.

Thomas McGuane's "Heart of the Game" has always meant something special to me, echoing my own feelings of the hunt. So has John Miller's "Deer Camp," which reminds me of my own hunting club in New York's Catskill Mountains, where 10 of us convene every November to live in a tar-paper shack and hunt whitetails along the Neversink River.

Everything written by Theodore Roosevelt and Jose Ortega y Gasset commands my attention. Their insights have lasted through the years, and for good reason. James R. Pierce's piece on old hunting buddies always stirs me, especially because I hunted with him for many years, and through his last season. And many may not know it, but Lee Wulff, world famous as a fisherman, was also a dedicated deer and bird hunter. I had the chance to hunt with Lee a number of times, and his observations on the natural world, both spoken and written, were unparalleled.

We have included other friends and acquaintances in this volume, not simply beause we know them, but because the people whom we often find ourselves around have as deep a feeling for the outdoors as we do. Tom McIntyre, Mark Sullivan, T. Edward Nickens, Lamar Underwood, and Ted Nugent have many differing opinions, yet each has the same respect for the animals we hunt.

The literature of hunting has always been a part of our heritage; it has helped form the foundation of this nation, our national psyche, and it keeps a great many of us going, staying anchored in a world that's becoming increasingly complex.

So as you make your way through these pages, take your time, study the words: They are there for a reason. Our hope is that they may hit home with you, that they may send you searching for books in your library as well.

—Jay Cassell,
Katonah, New York.
June 2011.

THE LITTLE RED BOOK OF
HUNTER'S WISDOM

● **Peter Fiduccia with bull moose, Newfoundland.**

PART ONE

ORIGINS AND METHODS

1

The Past

Strike ye our land with curved horns! Now with cries
bending our bodies, breathe fire upon us; now with feet
trampling the earth, let your hoofs thunder over us! The
buffalo I've taken and I lift up my voice; strike ye our land
with curved horns!
SIOUX BUFFALO CHANT (UNDATED)

• • •

We cannot but pity the boy who has never fired a gun; he
is no more humane, while his education has been sadly
neglected.
HENRY DAVID THOREAU
WALDEN (1854)

• • •

I have carried out my official duties as long and as faithfully as I can, and for the rest I have lived in such fashion as seemed most agreeable to me . . . convinced that a good day's shooting is second in point of pleasure to nothing else on earth.
LORD WARWICK, IN JONATHAN RUFFER'S
THE BIG SHOTS—EDWARDIAN SHOOTING PARTIES
(1977)

• • •

Of the strength and ferocity of the animal [grizzly bear] the Indians had given us dreadful accounts. They never attack him except in parties of six or eight persons, and even then are often defeated with a loss of one or more of their party.
MERIWETHER LEWIS AND WILLIAM CLARK
THE JOURNALS OF LEWIS AND CLARK (1805)

• • •

The pleasure of the sportsman in the chase is measured by the intelligence of the game and its capacity to elude pursuit and in the labor involved in the capture. It is a contest with sharp wits where satisfaction is mingled with admiration for the object overcome.
JOHN DEAN CATON
THE ANTELOPE AND DEER OF NORTH AMERICA (1877)

• • •

The legend of Lord Ripon rests simply on the fact that he could kill more birds than anybody else . . . At Sandringham he once killed twenty-eight pheasants in a minute. On another occasion he shot so quickly and accurately that he had seven birds dead in the air at once. His talents aroused some jealousy.

JONATHAN RUFFER

THE BIG SHOTS—EDWARDIAN SHOOTING PARTIES

(1977)

• • •

What of the hunting, hunter bold?
—Brother, the watch was long and cold.
What of the quarry ye went to kill?
—Brother, he crops in the jungle still.
Where is the power that made your pride?
—Brother, it ebbs from my flank and side.
Where is the haste that ye hurry by?
—Brother, I go to my lair to die.

RUDYARD KIPLING

"TIGER-TIGER," THE JUNGLE BOOKS (1894)

• • •

The caribou feeds the wolf, but it is the wolf who keeps the caribou strong.

KEEWATIN ESKIMO SAYING (UNDATED)

• • •

I can truthfully say I know of no other recreation that will do so much toward keeping a woman in good health and perfect figure than a few hours spent occasionally at trap shooting.
ANNIE OAKLEY
"ANNIE OAKLEY RULED THE TRAPS"
SPORTS AFIELD (AUGUST 1915)

• • •

Having prepared from the skin an apt resemblance of the living bird, they [Cherokee hunters] follow the turkey trails or haunts till they discover a flock, when they secrete themselves behind a log in such a manner to elude discovery, partially displaying their decoy and imitating the gobbling noise of the cock.
ALBERT HAZEN WRIGHT
EARLY RECORDS OF THE WILD TURKEY (1914)

• • •

It has always seemed to me that any man is a better man for being a hunter. This sport confers a certain constant alertness, and develops a certain ruggedness of character that, in these days of too much civilization, is refreshing; moreover, it allies us to the pioneer past. In a deep sense, this great land of ours was won for us by hunters.
ARCHIBALD RUTLEDGE
WHY I TAUGHT MY BOYS TO HUNT (EARLY 1940s)

• • •

Wilderness is the raw material out of which man has
hammered the artifact called civilization.
ALDO LEOPOLD
A SAND COUNTY ALMANAC (1949)

• • •

As all hunters, the people of the Americas relied on the skills
of stalking, tracking and trapping to get close to their quarry,
so the range and power of the weapon were not so important
as the craft of hunting.
ROBERT HARDY
LONGBOW: A SOCIAL AND MILITARY HISTORY (1976)

• • •

These bears, being so hard to die, rather intimidate us all. I
must confess that I do not like the gentlemen and had rather
fight two Indians than one bear. There is no other chance to
conquer them by a single shot but by shooting them through
the brains.
MERIWETHER LEWIS, *ALONG THE YELLOWSTONE*
(1805)

• • •

What is religious about hunting is that it leads us to
remember and accept the violent nature of our condition,
that every animal that eats will in turn one day be eaten. The
hunt keeps us honest.
DUDLEY YOUNG
ORIGINS OF THE SACRED (1991)

• • •

One morning . . . he heard a wild cacophony, a rumble
which seemed to move the earth yet came from the sky, and
he roused out to see descending toward his marsh a veritable
cloud of huge birds, all of them crying in loud voices, *"Onk-
or; onk-or!"* And in that first moment of seeing the geese
he comprehended them totally: jet-black head and neck,
snow-white underchin, beautiful cream body with brown
top, black tail, raucous, lovable, fat and constantly shouting
to each other, *"Onk-or!"*
JAMES A. MICHENER
CHESAPEAKE (1978)

• • •

Whoever consider themselves beautiful after seeing me has
no heart.
"SONG OF THE ELK", ACCORDING TO THE SIOUX ELK
SOCIETY, IN *DOG SOLDIERS, BEAR MEN AND BUFFALO
WOMEN*, BY THOMAS E. MAILS (1973)

• • •

2

The Joys of Hunting

Until you have courted bluebills in the snow, you have not
tasted the purer delights of waterfowling.
GORDON MACQUARRIE
*STORIES OF THE OLD DUCK HUNTERS & OTHER
DRIVEL* (1967)

• • •

He expected the wolf to come his way any moment. He made thousands of different conjectures as to where and from what side the beast would come and how he would set upon it. Hope alternated with despair. Several times he addressed a prayer to God that the wolf should come his way.

LEO TOLSTOY
WAR AND PEACE (1869)

• • •

Now it is pleasant to hunt something that you want very much over a long period of time, being outwitted, out-maneuvered, and failing at the end of each day, but having the hunt and knowing every time you are out that, sooner or later, your luck will change and that you will get the chance that you are seeking. But it is not pleasant to have a time limit by which you must get your kudu or perhaps never get it, nor even see one. It is not the way hunting should be.

ERNEST HEMINGWAY
GREEN HILLS OF AFRICA (1935)

• • •

In the joy of hunting is intimately woven the love of the great outdoors. The beauty of woods, valleys, mountains, and skies feeds the soul of the sportsman where the quest of game only whets his appetite.

DR. SAXTON POPE
HUNTING WITH THE BOW AND ARROW (1923)
[THE BOOK IS DEDICATED TO "ROBIN HOOD, A SPIRIT THAT AT SOME TIME DWELLS IN THE HEART OF EVERY YOUTH"]

• • •

At first glance the tree seemed alive with frantic squirrels. There appeared to be forty or fifty of them leaping and darting from branch to branch until the whole tree had become one green maelstrom of mad leaves.

WILLIAM FAULKNER
"THE BEAR" (1931)

• • •

The most and best is known to the man who quits his bed before sunrise . . . who spends his days on the mountains and forests who bears the heat and cold and hunger and thirst for the love of nature . . . to visit the utmost refuges of beast and bird.

ALFRED PEASE
BOOK OF THE LION (1987)

• • •

I'm Bully!
THEODORE ROOSEVELT, ON HOW HE FELT AFTER AN
ELEVEN-HOUR JAGUAR HUNT IN THE
JUNGLES OF BRAZIL (1914)

• • •

Although you may be out for game, the killing of game
should be only incidental, and you should be able calmly to
enjoy the beautiful scenery, the ever-changing lights on the
hills and forests and the game itself.
ELMER KEITH
BIG GAME HUNTING (1948)

• • •

. . . the Old Duck Hunters are extremely partial to the bitter
last days, those stormy days when the wild, free things of
duck shooting are abroad in the very wind with the storm.
GORDON MACQUARRIE
*STORIES OF THE OLD DUCK HUNTERS & OTHER
DRIVEL* (1967)

• • •

He came to the stream, and paused for a moment at the bridge. He wanted to tell them he was happy, if they only knew how happy he was, but when he opened his eyes he could not see them anymore. Everything else was bright but the room was dark.
COREY FORD
THE ROAD TO TINKHAMTOWN (1970)

• • •

I'm too intense about hunting. It's not a hobby. It's a lifestyle. It's a passion. So, I think almost without exception, both the men and the women I've known over the years who I've gotten along with best were outdoors people.
CHUCK ADAMS
LIFE AT FULL DRAW (2002)

• • •

The weather was already growing wintry and morning frosts congealed an earth saturated by autumn rains. The verdure had thickened and its bright green stood out sharply against the brownish strips of winter rye trodden down by the cattle, and against the pale-yellow stubble of the spring sowing and the reddish strips of buckwheat. The wooded ravines and the copses, which at the end of August had still been green islands amid black fields and stubble, had become golden and bright-red islands amid the green winter rye. The hares had already half changed their summer coats, the fox cubs were beginning to scatter, and the young wolves were bigger than dogs. It was the best time of the year for the chase.

LEO TOLSTOY
WAR AND PEACE (1869)

• • •

3

Skills

Get the best [rifle] that you can, of course; but do not worship it. Bear in mind that, whatever its trajectory and smashing quality, it is only a gun, and can kill nothing that you miss with it.

HORACE KEPHART

CAMPING AND WOODCRAFT (1917)

• • •

The placing of the bullet is everything.
COL. TOWNSEND WHELEN
MR. RIFLEMAN (WITH BRADFORD ANGIER) (1965)

• • •

In matters like hunting and fishing and falconry, mentors
are priceless. They teach you nuance, and detail, and what is
really important.
CHARLES FERGUS
THE UPLAND EQUATION (1995)

• • •

No, I'm not a good shot, but I shoot often
THEODORE ROOSEVELT (EARLY 1900s)
OLD EPHRAIM (1904)

• • •

Like most aspiring hunters, I was given, at an early age, a
single-barreled shotgun and permission to hunt rabbits.
ALDO LEOPOLD
RED LEGS KICKING (1946)

• • •

To the trapper-naturalist . . . the howl of the wolf . . . inspires
[a] challenge to his own skill as a hunter and trapper.
H. MCCRACKEN AND H. VAN CLEVE
*TRAPPING: THE CRAFT AND SCIENCE OF CATCHING
FUR-BEARING ANIMALS* (1947)

• • •

If one really wishes to be a master of an art, technical
knowledge is not enough. One has to transcend technique
so that art becomes an artless art growing out of the
unconscious. In the case of archery, the hitter and hit no
longer are two opposing objects, but are one reality.
DAISETZ T. SUZUKI
ZEN AND THE ART OF ARCHERY
TRANSLATED BY EUGEN HERRIGEL (1964)

• • •

The color of your clothes is not so important as many
hunters appear to think, for the background of Alaskan hills
in late autumn is a crazy-quilt of every violent color from
blood red to flame yellow—and anyway, it is motion rather
than form or color which catches sheep's eyes.
RUSSELL ANNABEL
*SPEAKING OF SHEEP HUNTING: TALES OF A BIG GAME
GUIDE* (1938)

• • •

Woodcraft may be defined as the art of finding one's way in the wilderness, and getting along well by utilizing Nature's storehouse.
HORACE KEPHART
CAMPING AND WOODCRAFT (1917)

• • •

The Johnny-come-latelies who followed us would not know the things we knew.
JOHN MYERS MYERS
THE WILD YAZOO (1947)

• • •

Every field archer should make his own tackle. If he can not make and repair it, he will never shoot very long, because it is in constant need of repair.
DR. SAXTON POPE
HUNTING WITH THE BOW AND ARROW (1923)

• • •

If a man's weapon is not dependable, then he is not dependable.
COL. TOWNSEND WHELEN
MR. RIFLEMAN (WITH BRADFORD ANGIER) (1965)

• • •

Every hunter has ultimately to learn the way himself . . .
The truest hunter must go beyond rote lessons to a degree of
knowledge that has become thoroughly ingrained, become
an instinctual quality of his being, something beyond mere
consciousness. He must, finally, be able to cross over from
understanding to knowing. That is what ultimately cannot
be taught.
THOMAS MCINTYRE
THE WAY OF THE HUNTER (1988)

• • •

Learning to hunt is not the same as learning to shoot even
though learning one certainly seems to help the other, and
it is hard to think of a good hunter who is not also a pretty
good shot.
RICHARD FORD
"HUNTING WITH MY WIFE"
SPORTS AFIELD (1996)

• • •

Any kind of hunting is fine with me, but I especially love to
go after whitetail deer with a bow. That's why I originally
started making bows years ago.
JIM HAMM
BOWS & ARROWS OF THE NATIVE AMERICANS (1989)

• • •

The successful bird hunter must be knowledgeable about many things but in the end it comes down to this: He must know his birds, his dogs, and his guns.
GEOFFREY NORMAN
THE ORVIS BOOK OF UPLAND BIRD SHOOTING (1985)

• • •

We all hunt in the fall—grouse, deer, elk, though we leave the moose and bear alone because they are not as common—but none of us is clever or stealthy enough to bowhunt. With a bow, you have to get close to the animal.
RICK BASS
IN THE LOYAL MOUNTAINS (1995)

• • •

I must have dozed, for my watch said eleven-thirty when I heard the first shot. It came with a pop, followed by an expanding wind, like a gale coming down a chimney toward me, out overhead and away toward the Dream River. And then another, perhaps eight, ten miles away. And finally a third. All from the same rifle. In the fallaway echo of that crack, the hairs on the back of my neck stiffened. I was being watched. I was sure of it.
MARK SULLIVAN
THE PURIFICATION CEREMONY (1997)

PART TWO

• • •

WHAT WE HUNT AND WHY

Game Animals, Waterfowl and Turkeys, Whitetail Deer, Big Game, Upland Birds, and Africa comprise this, the largest section of the book. By presenting observations on the animals themselves, from the past into the present, our aim is to give different insights into the animals we hunt. Perhaps some of the emotions that you have when afield are similar to those cited here. Perhaps you'll discover aspects to the game that you never considered before. Perhaps you'll discover bonds with those who came before us.

1

Game Animals

Whether in January or March, varying-hare hunting has a
singular appeal to those who like the woods to themselves.
NELSON BRYANT
*GOING AFTER THE VARYING HARE IN VERMONT'S
SNOW WOODS* (1990)

• • •

These days, of course, running bunnies with beagles has
more to do with the hunt and the hound music than filling
an empty belly, and modern rabbit hunters have definite—
and differing—ideas about what makes a good dog tick.
T. EDWARD NICKENS
"THE RABBIT RUNNERS," FIELD & STREAM
(OCTOBER 2004)

• • •

In a civilized and cultivated country, wild animals only
continue to exist at all when preserved by sportsmen.
The excellent people who protest against all hunting, and
consider sportsmen as enemies of wild life, are wholly
ignorant of the fact that in reality the genuine sportsman
is by all odds the most important factor in keeping wild
creatures from total extermination.
THEODORE ROOSEVELT (1905)

• • •

To my mind there is a peculiar fascination in hunting the
mule-deer. By the time hunting season has arrived the buck
is no longer the slinking beast of the thicket, but a bold and
yet wary dweller in the uplands.
THEODORE ROOSEVELT
OUTDOOR PASTIMES OF AN AMERICAN HUNTER
(1905)

• • •

For the wild animal there is no such thing as a gentle decline
in peaceful old age. Its life is spent at the front, in line of
battle, and as soon as its powers begin to wane in the least, its
enemies become too strong for it; it falls.
ERNEST THOMPSON SETON
LIVES OF THE HUNTED (1901)

• • •

There is one point on which I am convinced that all sportsmen—no matter whether their point of view has been a platform on a tree, the back of an elephant, or their own feet—will agree with me, and that is, that a tiger is a large-hearted gentleman with boundless courage and that when he is exterminated—as exterminated he will be unless public opinion rallies to his support—India will be the poorer by having lost the finest of her fauna.

JIM CORBEIT
MAN-EATERS OF KUMAON (1946)

• • •

It took me years to become at all proficient at stalking, shooting, knowing what the animals ate and where they spent the day hidden. The learning was sometimes confused, and generally took the form of an evolution.

CHARLES FERGUS
A ROUGH-SHOOTING DOG (1991)

• • •

There are other things much more important than game laws; but it will be a great mistake to imagine because until recently in Europe game laws have been administered in the selfish interest of one class and against the interest of the people as a whole, that here in this country, and under our institutions, they would not be beneficial to all our people. Far from game laws being in the interest of the few, they are emphatically in the interest
of the many.
THEODORE ROOSEVELT
THE DEER FAMILY (1902)

• • •

I usually point out to . . . youthful correspondents that in order to be a successful hunter they must know a great many things in addition to how and where to hunt. Particularly, they must know nature in all its phases, and they must be physically competent. I especially advise them to take up the study of biology and the natural sciences.
COL. TOWNSEND WHELEN
MR. RIFLEMAN (WITH BRADFORD ANGIER) (1965)

• • •

2

Waterfowl and Turkeys

To a real hunter the wild duck does not represent anything particularly fascinating, but owing to the absence for the time being of other game (this was at the beginning of September; woodcock had not yet arrived, and I'd become fed up with running over the fields after partridges), I heeded my hunter [guide] and set out for Lgov.

IVAN TURGENEV

THE HUNTING SKETCHES (1852)

• • •

The perils of duck hunting are great–especially for the duck.
WALTER CRONKITE

• • •

Outsiders call us sadists or masochists; sometimes both.
Others—mostly ourselves—describe our activities in
romantic, even heroic, terms. We take ourselves very
seriously and tend to forget that much of duck and goose
hunting is fun and sometimes ridiculous.
GEORGE REIGER
THE WINGS OF DAWN (1980)

• • •

Turkeys can be killed by chance, but when they are killed
consistently, it is not due to chance.
JOHN MCDANIEL
A SUCCESSFUL FALL HUNT (2000)

• • •

To watch mallards come in a flock, cut their wings and land
but a few feet in front of you on a cold winter day near
Stuttgart, Arkansas, is just about as close to heaven as I think
one can get on this Earth. And as one who believes, because
of my faith, that I'm going to Heaven, I'm pretty sure there
will be duck hunting in Heaven, and I can't wait.
MIKE HUCKABEE
NRA CONFERENCE (SEPTEMBER 2007)

• • •

I suppose it may seem like a strange sort of lullaby to some,
but I have never heard sweeter music than the muffled
report of duck guns on a distant marsh, and I know that
others share my feeling.
BURTON SPILLER
MORE GROUSE FEATHERS (1972)

• • •

While level flight is the rule, when necessary a duck can
perform any imaginable aerial maneuver, including any
found in a stunt flier's bag of tricks. Furthermore, it will
carry them out quicker, with more grace—and always come
out of them a whole duck!
EDGAR M. QUEENY
PRAIRIE WINGS (1946)

• • •

. . . if you have to be crazy to hunt ducks, I do not wish to
be sane.
ROBERT RUARK
"YOU GOT TO BE CRAZY TO BE A DUCK HUNTER"
IN *THE OLD MAN AND THE BOY* (1953)

• • •

Such is the depth of this [turkey] mystique, and so thick is the veil before the truth, that before the creature can even be approached with a modicum of reason and logic, it becomes necessary to peel away the layers of legend—much as one peels the skin from around an onion.

TOM KELLY
TENTH LEGION (1973)

• • •

Half a mile north of the pasture fence, his eye caught movement in the eastern sky. Slowly he lowered into a kneeling position, remembering what his dad had told him: "Sudden moves are always seen, but slow moves you might get away with."

CHARLES L. CADIEUX
GOOSE HUNTING (1979)

• • •

If you're like me, there are times when you wish that you were born about a century ago, born wealthy, and were a waterfowl hunter back when the ducks darkened the sun.

STEVE SMITH
HUNTING DUCKS AND GEESE (1984)

• • •

Any good shot will have his days when he is right and the
birds come easy.
RAY P. HOLLAND
SHOTGUNNING IN THE LOWLANDS (1945)

• • •

Dog-harried turkeys will make the angels weep.
TOM KELLY
TENTH LEGION (1973)

• • •

In those of us who derive enjoyment from the flight
of wildfowl and who know Arkansas' Grand Prairie, a
wistful nostalgia for its pin oak flats simmers and simmers
throughout spring and summer months. It boils over when
the first yellow leaf of autumn whispers that the Hunting
Winds are on their way.
EDGAR M. QUEENY
PRAIRIE WINGS (1946)

• • •

There are three reasons to take ducks home:
To eat.
To mount.
To be recognized by the Broom and Crockpot Club.
B. R. "BUCK" PETERSON
THE COMPLEAT WATERFO(U)WLER (1996)

• • •

All of the turkey's stealth and majesty go into making it the sport that it is. The kind that will have a man getting up three hours earlier than usual for four weeks running to go out into the woods when it is still dark and make a lot of strange noises, hoping to fool an unseen bird out there in the trees and gloom. Game that magnificent demands a level of commitment that borders on the obsessive and most turkey hunters are willing to make that commitment.

GEOFFREY NORMAN
THE ORVIS BOOK OF UPLAND BIRD SHOOTING (1985)

• • •

The companionships that can form in a refuge parking lot are the kind made of something good, and solid, and right— a belief in the sporting ethic and a fondness for the birds we hunt.

STEVE SMITH
HUNTING DUCKS AND GEESE (1984)

• • •

A wood duck place is, by definition, a special place. You go there alone, or with maybe one friend, and you don't go there often.

GRAY'S SPORTING JOURNAL (OCTOBER 1990)

• • •

Soul-wrenching is what distinguishes wildfowling from all
other shooting sports.
GEORGE REIGER
THE WILDFOWLER'S QUEST (1989)

• • •

I was standing in a swamp a while ago, looking at the teal
go through the dead gum trees. There were more in that
single flock than I'd ever seen at once before, and I shot one
out of the front of it, took the gun down, raised it and shot
a second from a third of the way through, and then put it
down again, and if I say I was content to watch the rest fly
past, I might actually mean I was too stunned by the size of
the mob to try reloading for a third.
RON FORSYTH
REFLECTIONS, MAN AND BOY (1997)

• • •

Essentially, there are ducks that are looking to set down, and
those who couldn't care less.
STEVE SMITH
HUNTING DUCKS AND GEESE (1984)

• • •

The blood of the modern waterfowler courses with heritage,
for we are ultimately the culmination of the people and
events that have shaped the sport we know today.
CHRlS DORSEY
WILDFOWLER'S SEASON (1995)

• • •

If you're a goose hunter, a dozen football-sized lumps of
blue clay with a piece of white paper stuck on each look like
a dozen lumps of blue clay . . . but if you're a blue or snow
goose, those lumps . . . must look like blue or snow geese,
and when you spot them from the air you may decide to pay
them a visit.
ED ZERN
HUNTING AND FISHING FROM "A" to ZERN (1985)

• • •

In a cynical and overcrowded world, the need for each of us
to cultivate a spiritual oasis shared with a few likeminded
friends is not readily perceived by the majority of people
numb with the mediocrity of modern life.
GEORGE REIGER
THE WILDFOWLER'S QUEST (1989)

• • •

The name turkey is sometimes said to have been given the bird because of confusion concerning the country of its origin. More probably it was suggested by the voice of the bird, as some of its calls sound like the syllables "turk-turk-turk—."

AUSTIN L. RAND
AMERICAN WATER AND GAME BIRDS (1956)

• • •

If you are one of those nervous, fidgety, head-rolling individuals who can't even sit still in a barber's chair, don't worry about duck blinds. You take up railbird shooting seriously and let the other fellow have the ducks.

RAY P. HOLLAND
SHOTGUNNING IN THE LOWLANDS (1945)

• • •

A turkey hunter operates in an austere, intellectual climate with a bare minimum of accessories—like one of those Japanese color prints of a single spray of blossoms. He grows accustomed to this stark simplicity, becomes fond of it . . .

TOM KELLY
BETTER ON A RISING TIDE (1995)

• • •

I find myself looking forward to fall, when Keewaydin, keeper of the mystic northland, unleashes the Hunting Winds. Then the subjects themselves will return, spread their wings in benediction over their haven in the color spotted flats, and rest and dabble in the solace of its tranquil waters—amidst the vast silence of its very vocal trees.

EDGAR M. QUEENY
PRAIRIE WINGS (1946)

• • •

Some of my fondest memories are tagging along in the woods with my father. At six I was deciphering turkey and deer sign. By eight I was a crack shot with my BB gun. I was 10 years old when I began toting a shotgun under Will Hanback's intense supervision. We didn't have many gobblers in Virginia back then, but that was okay. I was enjoying the woods with my father, and that is all that really mattered.

MICHAEL HANBACK
SPRING GOBBLER FEVER (1996)

• • •

To hunt ducks you must leave your comfortable, predictable surroundings for that less familiar place where ducks work their magic . . . their spell is cast only where they—not you—call home, and once there, you will refresh your soul and rediscover a simple passion.

B. R. "BUCK" PETERSON
THE COMPLAT WATERFO(U)WULER (1996)

• • •

I wonder whether I get closer to the core of things,
somehow, with a dog and a duck call I don't understand
why either of these should take me any closer to anywhere,
but that doesn't mean they don't take me there, I don't
understand why my dog retrieves with such zeal, but that's
no reason to stop using him.
RON FORSYTH
REFLECTIONS, MAN AND BOY (1997)

• • •

There is only one way to become a good duck caller. Get
someone who is really good to teach you, and then practice
year after year with domesticated mallards and with wild
ducks spring and fall. Stick to the mallard call at first.
RAY P. HOLLAND
SHOTGUNNING IN THE LOWLANDS (1945)

• • •

Bird hunting is companionable as deer hunting is solitary.
GEOFFREY NORMAN
THE ORVIS BOOK OF UPLAND BIRD SHOOTING (1985)

• • •

3

Whitetail Deer

As a trophy the whitetail leaves nothing to be desired.
Cannily outwitting all but the best (and luckiest) hunters—
many times, it seems, by divine guidance—when finally
taken he should be highly prized.
LAWRENCE R. KOLLER
SHOTS AT WHITETAILS (1948)

• • •

These are the names of the places I hunt: Buck Hill, the
Water Gap, the Burned-Off Hill, Camp Creek, the East Side,
the Back Side of Buck Hill, and Turkey Hollow.
RICK BASS
THE DEER PASTURE (1985)

• • •

The deerskin rug on our study floor, the buck's head over the fireplace, what are these after all but the keys which have unlocked enchanted doors, and granted us not only health and vigor, but a fresh and fairer vision of existence.

PAUL BRANDRETH
TRAILS OF ENCHANTMENT (1930)

• • •

Whitetail Deer

The serious here are of two kinds. Those who hunt deer and those who hunt turkeys. By far the overwhelming number of disciples that follow either of these two religions follow that of deer hunting.

TOM KELLY
TENTH LEGION (1973)

• • •

They are likely to die in March. And they die unmourned,
untended, unnoted.
CURTIS STADTFELD
WHITETAIL DEER (1975)

• • •

It is generally agreed that anyone who can successfully hunt
these wily animals will have little trouble with other game.
FRED BEAR
FRED BEAR'S WORLD OF ARCHERY (1979)

• • •

He is alone, his eye, focused on the track, follows its
threaded imprint out through the hallways and blow-downs
ahead, as far as his eye can see. His eye searches for an ear, an
outline—a suggestion of gray-brown where an animal stands
motionless . . . watching.
JOHN RANDOLPH
"HAWK WHO WALKS HUNTING" IN *SEASONS OF THE
HUNTER*
EDITED BY ELMAN AND SEYBOLD (1985)

• • •

. . . there's little manhood in killing a doe, and that, too, out
of season.
JAMES FENIMORE COOPER
NATTY BUMPPO, IN *THE DEERSLAYER* (1842)

• • •

Whether or not I really want to kill the buck, I am not yet
willing to forego the company of men who hunt.
JAMES KILGO
DEEP ENOUGH FOR IVORYBILLS (1988)

• • •

Hunting must be a love affair when, beyond all other
emotions, the desire to possess rules. One must reach out
for what one cannot quite understand. Whatever animal
becomes ordinary must be allowed to pass by. The sight of a
magnificent buck I want to feel at a close range. To want to
kill him with any less intensity seems murderous to me . . . .
HARRISON O'CONNOR
"HUNTING ON THE FARM"
GRAY'S SPORTING JOURNAL (1984)

• • •

The first American is not really a Puritan, Thanksgiving notwithstanding. He's not really a Christian with starched collar and blunderbuss. And he's not a Thomas Jefferson, the Fourth of July notwithstanding, with his intellect and his words. He's a [deer] hunter with a Kentucky long rifle and a long knife, and he's gone more or less native. And he first comes to us fighting with a judge over a carcass of a Christmas deer.

CHARLES BERGMAN

ORION'S LEGACY: A CULTURAL HISTORY OF MAN AS HUNTER (1996)

• • •

Deer stands have a magnetic attraction for any deer hunter. He learns from his pals that many deer have been killed from Patterson's Rock or the Twin-Oak Stand or Skunk-Gully; he swells mentally in anticipation as he approaches any of these hallowed spots, knowing that when the drive comes through, his chances of killing that whitetail buck are better than those of the unfortunates who may be watching less favored areas. Every deer club has these sacred spots, and sacred they are, indeed. They have achieved reputations simply because deer favor these places for moving from hideout to hideout.

LARRY KOLLER

SHOTS AT WHITETAILS (1948)

• • •

I crave no cloth better than the skin of a deer, nor any meat richer than his flesh. Well may you call it strong! Strong it is, and strong it make him who eats it!
NATTY BUMPPO
"THE LEATHERSTOCKING TALES,"
JAMES FENIMORE COOPER, (1823–1841)

• • •

No species of wild animal inhabiting North America deserves to be regarded with more interest than the common Virginian Deer; its symmetrical form, graceful curving leap or bound, and its rushing speed, when flying before its pursuers, it passes like a meteor by the startled traveler in the forest, exciting admiration, though he be ever so dull an observer.
AUDUBON/BACHMAN
THE QUADRUPEDS OF NORTH AMERICA (1848)

• • •

I stalk through life like a deer.
A GERMAN DEERSLAYER CALLED "MILLER" IN AN
UNPUBLISHED LETTER (OCTOBER 16,1838)

• • •

When we came within sight of the deer, the canoe was allowed to float down with the current, and the steersman laid it in a position the most advantageous for those who were in the bow with guns. The deer would generally raise their heads and stand looking . . . until the canoe came within a few yards of them.
PHILIP TOME (EARLY 1800s)

• • •

Whether he swam the Combahee, as he had before he swam the Chee-ha; whether he here escaped from the hounds, or was devoured by them; whether he was a deer of flesh and blood, or the phantom buck of legend—we cannot decide.
WILLIAM ELLIOTT
CAROLINA SPORTS BY LAND AND WATER (1846)

• • •

For durability, buckskin is as important as it is to the hero of a sporting romance."
T.S. VAN DYKE (1882)

• • •

The deerskin on our sturdy floor, the buck's head over the fireplace, what are these after all but the keys which have unlocked enchanted doors and granted us not only health and vigor, but a fresh and fairer vision of existence?
PAUL BRANDRETH
TRAILS OF ENCHANTMENT (1930)

• • •

Although being lost in the woods is, at best, an unpleasant experience, thousands of deer hunters contrive to do it every year.
NELSON BRYANT
"FINDING YOUR WAY IN THE WOODS" (1990)

• • •

In the American South, deer hunting in particular verges on an organized religion. . . . It is a hobby that often borders on an obsession, and is particularly entrenched in the Mississippi Delta.
ALAN HUFFMAN
TEN POINT: DEER CAMP IN THE MISSISSIPPI DELTA (1977)

• • •

Then the buck was there. He did not come into sight; he was just there, looking not like a ghost but as if all of the light were condensed in him and he were the source of it, not only moving in it but disseminating it, already running, seen first as you always see the deer, in that split second after he has already seen you, already slanting away in that first soaring bound, the antlers even in that dim light looking like a small rocking-chair balanced on his head.

WILLIAM FAULKNER
"THE OLD PEOPLE,"
HARPER'S MONTHLY, (SEPTEMBER 1940)

• • •

Alone in the mountains I hunt,
Wandering amazed at my own lightness and glee,
In the late afternoon choosing a safe spot to pass the night,
Kindling a fire and broiling the fresh-kill'd game,
Falling asleep on the gather'd leaves with my dog and gun by my side.

WALT WHITMAN
"SONG OF MYSELF" (1860)

• • •

The whitetail deer is now, and we hope always will be, the
big game of the common man.
LAWRENCE R. KOLLER
SHOTS AT WHITETAILS (1948)

• • •

I'm a jeep man. The deer pasture is a jeep place.
RICK BASS
THE DEER PASTURE (1985)

• • •

I think if you'd like to renew your acquaintance with
yourself, you could do worse than spend time on a deer
stand. Sometimes the hours go quickly, and you become part
of the scene. Sometimes each half-minute is torture . . .
DAVID MAMET
"DEER HUNTING"
MEN'S JOURNAL (1994)

• • •

The whitetail is the most beautiful and graceful of all our
game animals when in motion.
THEODORE ROOSEVELT
THE DEER FAMILY (1902)

• • •

To go deer hunting, the archer should seek a country
unspoiled by civilization and gunpowder.
DR. SAXTON POPE
HUNTING WITH THE BOW AND ARROW (1923)

• • •

By the time a buck is truly mature and therefore possibly in
the trophy class, his habits and patterns of movement have
become so different from those of ordinary deer that he
evades common hunting methods effortlessly.
JOHN WOOTERS
HUNTING TROPHY DEER (1997)

• • •

The whitetail is the American Deer of the past, and the
American Deer of the future.
ERNEST THOMPSON SETON
LIVES OF GAME ANIMALS (1929)

• • •

In discussing deer hunting as a sport, it seems to me that we must never lose sight of the fact that its interest is due chiefly to the nature of the game pursued . . . I hope to be a stag follower as long as I can see a sight. This feeling I attribute to the character of the deer—that noble, elusive, crafty, wonderful denizen of the wilds, the pursuit of which is surely the master sport of the huntsman.

ARCHIBALD RUTLEDCE
DAYS OFF IN DIXIE (1924)

• • •

Orange is the color of November in Michigan. Not the soft orange of aspen or maple, for the leaves have already fallen. I mean the harsh fluorescence of blaze orange that glows along the country roads and in the little towns up north on the fifteenth of the month.

JOHN MITCHELL
THE HUNT (1979)

• • •

I will always be impressed by the species' ability to survive such unbelievable hardship at the northern edge of their geographic range.

JOHN OZOGA
WHITETAIL COUNTRY (1992)

• • •

The deer hunter of experience wastes no time in watching
barren ground.
LAWRENCE R. KOLLER
SHOTS AT WHITETAILS (1948)

• • •

The alarm clock goes off at 4 AM after a long Friday night of
poker and reacquaintances at the Coventry Gore Liar's Club,
a hunting camp in the hills behind town. My body moves
sluggishly.
JOHN MILLER
DEER CAMP (1992)

• • •

Unbelievable. My [six-year-old] son had found the antler
of the buck I had hunted, unsuccessfully, all season. The big
10-pointer I had seen the day before deer season, the one
with the wide spread and thick beams.
JAY CASSELL
"THE RACK"
SPORTS AFIELD (1992)

• • •

No mammal in the world has likely attracted more attention, stirred more controversy, or has been so intensively investigated as the adaptable white-tailed deer (*Odocoileus virginianus*), a species that has not only survived in the wake of modern man's devastation, but has thrived and greatly expanded its traditional range in the Americas.
JOHN OZOGA
WHITETAIL COUNTRY (1992)

• • •

I'm invisible. At least I hope so. I'd better be, since I plan to get within arrow range of a whitetail deer.
JIM HAMM
BOWS & ARROWS OF THE NATIVE AMERICANS (1989)

• • •

Halloween brings us closer.
RICK BASS
IN THE LOYAL MOUNTAINS (1995)

• • •

Use common sense when hunting deer. The most successful whitetail hunters constantly apply heavy doses of good ol' common sense about deer to their deer hunting strategies.
PETER J. FIDUCCIA
WHITETAIL STRATEGIES (1995)

• • •

Any sportsman who can kill his deer without the tingling spine, the quick clutch at his heart, the delicious trembling of nerve fibers when the game is finally down, has no place in the deer woods.
LAWRENCE R. KOLLER
SHOTS AT WHITETAILS (1948)

• • •

4

Big Game

In the West, generally, I think, the lion is considered cowardly—a belief I share, though agreeing with Theodore Roosevelt, who in "The Wilderness Hunter" says cougars, and, in fact, all animals vary in moods just as much as mankind. Because of their feline strategy and craftiness, they are most difficult animals to hunt; I know none more so.

CASPER W. WHITNEY
"THE COUGAR" IN *HUNTING IN MANY LANDS*
EDITED BY ROOSEVELT AND GRINNELL (1895)

• • •

The wolf is by nature cowardly, being deficient in courage comparative to his strength and great size, but he often becomes courageous from necessity.
ROGER D. WILLIAMS
''WOLF-COURSING'' IN *HUNTING IN MANY LANDS*
EDITED BY ROOSEVELT AND GRINNELL (1895)

• • •

The razorback has a mind of his own; not instinct, but mind . . . He thinks. He bears grudges, broods over indignities, and plans redress for the morrow or the week after. If he cannot get even with you, he will lay for your unsuspecting friend.
HORACE KEPHART
OUR SOUTHERN HIGHLANDERS (1917)

• • •

I will still his mighty bugle if it is willed. I'll claim him as a trophy if my puny arrow flies true. But he will always be the unattainable; with the mountain, the fog, and the silent stones.
BILLY ELLIS
HUNTER TO THE DAWN (1988)

• • •

The pleasure of the sportsman in the chase is measured by the intelligence of the game and its capacity to elude pursuit and in the labor involved in the capture. It is a contest with sharp wits where satisfaction is mingled with admiration for the object overcome.

JUDGE JOHN DEAN CATON
THE ANTELOPE AND DEER OF NORTH AMERICA (1877)

• • •

The true trophy hunter is a self-disciplined perfectionist seeking a single animal, the ancient patriarch well past his prime that is often an outcast from his own kind . . . If successful, he will enshrine the trophy in a place of honor. This is a more noble and fitting end than dying on some lost and lonely ledge where the scavengers will pick his bones, and his magnificent horns will weather away and be lost forever.

ELGIN GATES
TROPHY HUNTER IN ASIA (1971)

• • •

The elk of a lifetime reminds us that the value of the hunt cannot be measured in inches.

E. DONNALL THOMAS, JR.
TWO BULLS (1997)

• • •

By now he knew the old bear's footprint better than he did his own, and not only the crooked one.
WILLIAM FAULKNER
"THE BEAR" (1931)

• • •

Tigers do not know that human beings have no sense of smell, and when a tiger becomes a man-eater it treats human beings exactly as it treats wild animals, that is, it approaches its intended victims up-wind, or lies up in wait for them down-wind.
JIM CORBETT
MAN-EATERS OF KUMAON (1946)

• • •

Now the familiar cries of the birds told him what the wind could not: the two-legged creatures were still coming— and they were very near. To strike them down, he would need the wind.
LAMAR UNDERWOOD
ON DANGEROUS GROUND (1989)

• • •

A wolf killed with a firearm represents one of the most prized trophies.
CLYDE ORMOND
THE COMPLETE BOOK OF HUNTING (1962)

• • •

Three bear carcasses hung from the meat racks, skinned. A skinned bear looks eerily like a human being. I didn't know that until then.
PETER FROMM
INDIAN CREEK CHRONICLES (1993)

• • •

For all the time that I'd been in the forest I was hunting my first panther. But over and above this was the knowledge that here was combat as well as hunting. My rifle held one bullet. Should the furious, cornered animal charge toward me I had one chance only to stop him.
JOHN MYERS MYERS
THE WILD YAZOO (1947)

• • •

More than most American game animals, the pronghorn, by
virtue of the terrain he inhabits, is genuinely the rifleman's
quarry of choice.
THOMAS McINTYRE
DREAMING THE LION (1993)

• • •

In sheep hunting, good binoculars and the ability to use
them are more important than the rifle and cartridge and
generally, but by no means always, more important even
than shooting skill.
JACK O'CONNOR
IN *OUTDOOR LIFE* (1960)

• • •

5

Upland Birds

The more I see of the people's representatives, the more
I like my dogs.
COMTE ALFRED D'ORSAY (1850)

• • •

Your heart grows tired of waiting, and suddenly—but
only sportsmen will understand me—suddenly in the deep
stillness there comes a special kind of whirr and swish, you
hear the measured stroke of swift wings—and the woodcock,
with his long beak drooping gracefully down, comes
swimming out from a dark birch tree to meet your fire.
This is what is meant by "waiting for the flight."
IVAN TURGENEV
A SPORTSMAN'S NOTEBOOK (1850)

• • •

The idea is not to look for pheasants, plural and abstract, but pheasant: a singular, particular, concrete cock pheasant. You have to find them one by one, not collectively. Consider it a kind of big-game hunting.

DATUS PROPER
INTELLIGENCE (1991)

• • •

There are only two times of year in Montana: bird season and all the rest.

E. DONNALL THOMAS
"AUTUMN QUARTER," BIG SKY JOURNAL (FALL 2000)

• • •

Isn't there a time or two you can remember when somehow an animal you've hunted has done something to make you let him vanish in the woods? . . . Isn't there a bird or covey that somehow always manages to catch you with your gun on safe—even when you know it's there? I think we all know times that for almost certain we gave the hunt to the quarry.

GENE HILL
MOSTLY TAILFEATHERS (1975)

• • •

She was struck more and more powerfully, more and more definitely, by their scent; suddenly it became perfectly clear to her that one of them was right there, behind that hummock, five steps in front of her; she halted and her whole body grew rigid. Her short legs made it impossible for her to see anything in front of her, but by the smell she could tell it was not more than five steps away. She stood there, more and more aware of its presence and enjoying the anticipation. Her rigid tail was outstretched, only its very tip twitching. Her mouth was lightly open and her ears pricked up. One of her ears had got folded back while she was running; she was breathing heavily, but cautiously, and she looked round her still more cautiously, more with her eyes than with her head, at her master. He, with his familiar face, and eyes that were always so terrifying, came stumbling over the hummocks, it seemed to her extraordinarily slowly. It appeared to her that he was walking slowly, though he was running.

LEO TOLSTOY
ANNA KARENINA (1877)

• • •

A few fallen woodcock may be located without a dog, but to shoot those delightful little birds other than over a pointing dog would be like drinking Château Haut-Brion from a paper cup.

GEORGE BIRD EVANS
AN AFFAIR WITH GROUSE (1982)

• • •

The land comes alive through its wild creatures. I come to know the land through hunting the birds. Hunting has opened the earth to me and let me sense the rhythms and hierarchies of nature.

CHARLES FERGUS
THE UPLAND EQUATION (1995)

• • •

Dogs, even the most cross-grained, will tolerate all manner of liberties on the part of a pup. He is the privileged character in any kennel—until he attains his maturity. Then the others expect him to put away childish things.

HAVILAH BABCOCK
"WHEN DOGS FIGHT" IN
MY HEALTH IS BETTER IN NOVEMBER (1947)

• • •

After all has been said and done, when it comes to native wariness, individual daring and resourcefulness, power, cunning and all those things that place one creature above another, physically and mentally, then we must turn to our native pa'tridge. I should say our native grouse, as known to those who have seen him at his best. He is the king of American game birds and so those who have hunted them all will attest.

WILLIAM HARNDEN FOSTER
NEW ENGLAND GROUSE SHOOTING (1947)

• • •

The woodcock is a living refutation of the theory that the utility of a game bird is to serve as a target, or to pose gracefully on a slice of toast . . . Since learning of the sky dance, I find myself calling one or two birds enough. I must be sure that, come April, there will be no dearth of dancers in the sunset sky. . . .

ALDO LEOPOLD
A SAND COUNTY ALMANAC (1949)

• • •

But what was lovely was the fall to go hunting through the chestnut woods. The birds were all good because they fed on grapes and you never took a lunch because the peasants were always honored if you would eat with them at their houses.

ERNEST HEMINGWAY
A FAREWELL TO ARMS (1929)

• • •

If there be two things on earth, which, to be done *well*, must be done *young*, they are to shoot on the wing, and to ride across-country. They cannot be learned old, more than it can "to speak the truth."

FRANK FORESTER (1807–1858)

• • •

For all that I, for one, am never overeager to visit him, and if it were not for the grouse and the partridge, I should probably have dropped his acquaintance altogether.

IVAN TURGENEV
A HUNTER'S SKETCHES (1852)

• • •

I hunted with Dad for two years before I took my first shot
at a flying grouse or woodcock. Just about every autumn
weekend I trailed behind him through the thickest, muckiest
terrain in New Hampshire, following, literally, in his
footsteps, as I would metaphorically through much of my
life. I did not carry a gun. I watched and learned, and while
he did all the shooting, I did hunt.

WILLIAM G. TAPPLY
SPORTSMAN'S LEGACY (1993)

• • •

We can kill a big male sage grouse and feel his improbable
weight (there is no better definition of specific density than a
brace of mature sage roosters, three or four hot miles from a
pickup), and smell his acrid blood, like railroad ties on a hot
day, but the birds will always remain strangers. No, let me
correct that. We will always remain strangers in their land.

JOHN BARSNESS
WESTERN SKIES (1994)

• • •

The fact that the improvement of my health coincides with
the advent of quail season doesn't mean that my ills during
the rest of the year are imaginary. For outdoor pursuits have
a recognized therapeutic value. Especially quail hunting.
HAVILAH BABCOCK
MY HEALTH IS BETTER IN NOVEMBER (1947)

• • •

Though I have flushed many a covey of quail I have never
become used to it.
AUSTIN L. RAND
AMERICAN WATER AND GAME BIRDS (1956)

• • •

What I wanted, what I demanded from my dog, was the
loving, savage partnership of the hunt.
CHARLES FERGUS
A ROUGH-SHOOTING DOG (1991)

• • •

I would not lend my dog to a better sportsman than myself—because no two sportsmen hunt their dogs, as I have observed, exactly alike, and I wish my dog to hunt as I want him to hunt, not better than he does, nor worse.
FRANK FORESTER (1808-1858)

• • •

Whatever the unquestioned merits of the auto-loader and the repeater are in other branches of shotgun work, they are too clumsy, poorly lined and generally too heavy to be given place in the class of real grouse guns.
WILLIAM HARNDEN FOSTER
NEW ENGLAND GROUSE SHOOTING (1947)

• • •

Among all the upland gamebirds the sportsman rates the ruffed grouse as "king."
AUSTIN L. RAND
AMERICAN WATER AND GAME BIRDS (1956)

• • •

A friend once burned up three boxes of shells to bag one [pheasant] rooster. To put it mildly, he found that frustrating. Just into his fourth box he missed another rooster at eight paces. Uttering a sulphurous oath, he whipped his expensive cowboy hat into the sky and touched off a shot. And wouldn't you know, he shredded the hat, which was a tougher shot than any of those roosters that got away.
STEVE GROOMS
PHEASANT HUNTER'S HARVEST (1990)

• • •

My observations led me to believe there is nothing about the human figure that will alarm a ruffed grouse as long as the figure is motionless.
BURTON SPILLER
MORE GROUSE FEATHERS (1938)

• • •

I am aware that a number of staid and conservative citizens in my community look upon me as a fit candidate for an asylum. They argue, and perhaps rightly, that any middle-aged man who spends two months of each year in chasing a bird dog around through the woods has something far more serious the matter with him than mere eccentricity.

BURTON SPILLER
MORE GROUSE FEATHERS (1938)

• • •

While they [the shooters] were both talking, Laska, pricking up her ears, looked up at the sky, and then at them, full of reproach. Now's the time they've found for chattering, she thought, and here they come flying . . . yes, there it is, they'll miss it, thought Laska.

LEO TOLSTOY
ANNA KARENINA (1877)

• • •

The prettiest thing in the art of shooting, and that which is the result of the highest skill and practice so that it may be regarded as nearly the perfection of sportsmanship, is the killing double-shots accurately, cleanly, and in fine dashing style.
FRANK FORESTER (1807-1858)

• • •

It is the ruffed grouse (and its migratory sidekick, the woodcock) that makes dedicated wastrels of so many hunting men in the mixed hardwood forests of the Northeast.
JOHN MITCHELL
THE HUNT (1979)

• • •

Old gun dogs have stood the test of time and event and circumstance. They come now, slowly, and lay at foot or close to side, jowls flat, eyes faded with the fog of cataract, their muzzles and paws white or speckled salt and pepper. But they come. They want to be close. They are great treasures, these old dogs. For they are more than themselves lying there. They are us.
BILL TARRANT
IN *FIELD & STREAM* (1983)

• • •

There are covers I don't like to hunt except with certain people.
CRAIG WOODS
"THE ENDLESS COVER" IN *SEASONS OF THE HUNTER*
EDITED BY ELMAN AND SEYBOLD (1985)

• • •

In the morning we were in the covert, first thing. The wind had dropped in the night. Frost sparkled on the brambles, and the creek's steamy breath had whitened the willow boughs. The earth sucked at my boots. The shotgun hulls slipped in easily. I stuck the whistle between my teeth . . .
CHARLES FERGUS
A ROUGH-SHOOTING DOG (1991)

• • •

The successful hunter of any game is not necessarily the best marksman, but rather one who thoroughly understands his quarry, and I learned to know grouse in those days as but few of the younger generation will ever have a chance to know them.
BURTON SPILLER
MORE GROUSE FEATHERS (1938)

• • •

I love to kill those pheasants and eat their savage breasts.
JOHN BARSNESS
WESTERN SKIES (1994)

• • •

As forecast, the night brought a slight layer of snow. Today will be my final hunt for grouse this year: the gamecover is skinny, its feed depleted, and the scent's worse and worse in the cold. Of course, I have the flu.
SYDNEY LEA
HUNTING THE WHOLE WAY HOME (1994)

• • •

I may shoot fifty dove a season; guests sometimes shoot two hundred more. That sounds like a lot until you learn that more mourning dove are shot each year in the United States than all other migratory game birds combined.
GEORGE REIGER
HERON HILL CHRONICLE (1994)

• • •

I dream about my dogs, but recently the dreams have been turning to nightmares.
GUY DE LA VALDENE
FOR A HANDFUL OF FEATHERS (1995)

• • •

Each time we kill a bird, we die a little ourselves, and in that death renew our love for what we've killed.
ROBERT F. JONES
IT WOULDN'T BE THE SAME (1996)

• • •

The gardener . . . complains of its [the pheasant's] depredations on a wide variety of truck crops and growing corn, but in view of this splendid game bird's widespread popularity some disadvantages must be tolerated and local remedies sought.
AUSTIN L. RAND
AMERICAN WATER AND GAME BIRDS (1956)

• • •

He knelt beside the dog on dry ground at the edge of the
alders and put his arm around the dog's neck. Take it slow
and easy through here. Work it good. They hold tight this
early in the season, most or em will. They haven't been
hunted yet. All right?
ROBERT F. JONES
DANCERS IN THE SUNSET SKY (1996)

• • •

"Shoot 'em," says the girl, with a good laugh under a tossing
head. "They like to hang in the stubble beyond the barn, by
that culvert over there." . . . The swirls of pheasant tails are
everywhere in the snow, the little foot scratchings, like white
tattoos . . . Call me Ishmael, we eat blubber tonight.
STEVE CHAPPLE
CONFESSIONS OF AN ECO-REDNECK (1997)

• • •

Sweetzer was having REM dreams in the bunk after her day's
work, eyes rolling back in her head, legs twitching, nose
working, muscles rippling beneath her sleek coat. She was
probably still hunting . . .
JIM FERGUS
A HUNTER'S ROAD (1992)

• • •

6

Africa

Man . . . can understand a lion, because a lion is life in
its simplest form, beautiful, menacing, dangerous, and
attractive to his ego. A lion has always been the symbol of
challenge, the prototype of personal hazard. You get the lion,
or the lion gets you.
ROBERT RUARK
USE ENOUGH GUN (1952)

• • •

. . . the sparkling torrential rains, the sweeping thunderstorms, the grass fires creeping over the veld at night like snakes of living flame, the glorious aspect of the heavens, now of a spotless blue, now charged with the splendid and many-coloured lights of sunset, and now sparkling with a myriad stars, the wine-like taste of the air upon the plains, the beautiful flowers in the bushclad *kloofs*—all these things impressed me, so much that were I to live a thousand years I never should forget them.

H. RIDER HAGGARD
AUTOBIOGRAPHY (1925)

• • •

The chance of shooting—over a kill—an animal that has in all probability become a man-eater through a wound received over a kill, is very remote, and each succeeding failure, no matter what its cause, tends to make the animal more cautious, until it reaches a state when it either abandons its kill after one meal or approaches it as silently and as slowly as a shadow, scanning every leaf and twig with the certainty of discovering its would-be slayer, no matter how carefully he may be concealed or how silent and motionless he may be; a one in a million chance of getting a shot, and yet, who is there among us who would not take it?

JIM CORBETT
THE THAK MAN-EATER (1944)

• • •

Cape buffalo do not bluff a charge. When one of them comes at you, he's not voicing an opinion—he wants to meet you personally.
PHILIP CAPUTO
"SHADOWS IN THE BUSH," FIELD & STREAM (JULY 2005)

• • •

I knew, coldly and outside myself, that I could shoot a rifle on game as well as any son of a bitch that ever lived. Like hell I could.
ERNEST HEMINGWAY
GREEN HILLS OF AFRICA (1935)

• • •

I am one of the last of the old-time hunters. The events I saw can never be relived. Both the game and the native tribes, as I knew them, are gone. No one will ever see again the great elephant herds led by old bulls carrying 150 lb of ivory in each tusk. No one will ever hear again the yodelling war cries of the Masai as their spearmen swept the bush after cattle-killing lions. Few indeed will be able to say they have broken into country never before seen by a white man. No, the old Africa has passed, and I saw it go.
JOHN A. HUNTER (1952)
IN *SAFARI: A CHRONICLE OF ADVENTURE*
BY BARTLE BULL (1988)

• • •

A wounded leopard is both cunning and fierce. Once hit, he will dart into the thickest available cover and lie low. If he perceives that conditions are favorable, he will not hesitate to charge. Often he lets the hunter approach to within a few yards before revealing himself, and then, at the last moment, makes a lightning dash for his pursuer.

JAMES MELLON
AFRICAN HUNTER (1975)

• • •

A very small minority of the sportsmen who journey to Africa today to hunt have any skill whatever in rifle marksmanship. Most are utterly unable to place their shots with precision. Riflemen are made, not born. Moreover, unless a man has considerable skill with and reliance in his weapon, he will not remain cool in the presence of dangerous game close by . . . Thus, for both safety and success it is very necessary for all present-day hunters to employ the heavier calibers of modern rifles for such dangerous game, namely those of at least .416 bore or larger . . .
COL. TOWNSEND WHELEN, SOMEDAY FARM, WOODSTOCK,
VERMONT (1960)

• • •

In my experience haste in firing and flinch are the commonest causes of spoilt or inadequate shots; I mean those requiring one or more subsequent shots to kill outright. I myself am naturally of a rather highly strung nature and I suffered greatly from the eagerness that so easily leads to abortive shots. I found that if I kept in good training bodily and forced myself to count ten slowly I then brought off many good shots and a few brilliant ones.
W. D. M. "KARAMOJO" BELL
ON RIFLES AND SHOOTING (1950)

• • •

I speak of Africa and golden joys; the joy of wandering through lonely lands; the joy of hunting the mighty and terrible lords of the wilderness, the cunning, the wary and the grim.
THEODORE ROOSEVELT, IN KHARTOUM
(MARCH 15, 1910)

• • •

The leopard had bitten through my left arm, breaking it above the elbow with a crunch I can still hear. My mauled arms and hands burned as if dipped in acid. Some people say that serious injuries leave a fellow numb and shocked but not in severe pain. With me it was just the opposite. There's an old Chinese torture called the"death of a thousand cuts"—well, I know what that feels like.
ERIC RUNDGREN
"MY FIRST LEOPARD MAULING" IN
AFRICAN HUNTER BY JAMES MELLON (1975)

• • •

Nothing in the war terrified me so much as walking up to my first elephant, and I was reasonably terrified during the war.
ROBERT RUARK
IN *TRUE* (SEPTEMBER 1963)

• • •

I would place Old Jumbo on top of the list of big game and also as the most dangerous. When hunting elephants you are up against an intelligence not found in any other animal. Tembo lives to a very old age, probably considerably greater than the average span of man, and he learns as he lives.
ELMER KEITH
AFRICA'S BIG FIVE (1960)

• • •

I had loved country all my life; the country was always better than the people. I could only care about a very few people at a time.
ERNEST HEMINGWAY
GREEN HILLS OF AFRICA (1935)

• • •

For the most part man gets on with crocodiles about as well as he did with dragons; he will banish them from all but the remotest parts of the earth.
PETER BEARD AND ALISTAIR GRAHAM
EYELIDS OF MORNING (1974)

• • •

In a serious charge, the elephant comes quietly and at full speed, his trunk lowered and ears pressed tight against his head. In which case be prepared to shoot or to run the three-minute mile.
JAMES MELLON
AFRICAN HUNTER (1975)

• • •

When you've hunted big game for several decades all over the world, you take for granted occasional discomfort and even hardship. But dangerous situations arise very seldom, and when they do, it is nearly always the upshot of folly. Nine times out of ten, when an animal injures a hunter, it's because the hunter has bungled. But that tenth time, all your skill and experience count for exactly nothing.

DR. W. BRANDON MACOMBER
"A DOUBLE LION MAULING" IN
AFRICAN HUNTER BY JAMES MELLON (1975)

• • •

I don't know what there is about buffalo that frightens me so. Lions and leopards and rhinos excite me but don't frighten me. But the buff is so big and mean and ugly and hard to stop, and vindictive and cruel and surly and ornery. He looks like he hates you personally. He looks like you owe him money. He looks like he is hunting you.

ROBERT RUARK
HORN OF THE HUNTER (1954)

• • •

If a herd [of giant eland] runs away, you often have to chase the animals on foot for a half mile or so, until they stop to look back. And it's not so easy to shoot offhand at an animal standing two hundred yards away in a big herd, when you've just run several hundred yards yourself and are gasping for breath. You know that if you miss, maybe another two weeks will go by and you'll walk a hundred and fifty miles more before getting another crack at one.

JAMES MELLON
AFRICAN HUNTER (1975)

PART THREE

• • •

LOGIC OF HUNTING

Why We Hunt, The Essence of Hunting, Afield, and Etcetera finish off *The Little Red Book of Hunter's Wisdom*. Why We Hunt and The Essence will make you think, become a bit introspective, perhaps make you examine your own motives, admire those of others. Afield is a compendium of notes from the fields and woods, observations by the various authors. Etcetera is just that; a "they said it" section, with passages that reflect on certain aspects of hunting but simply don't fit anywhere else. Some of the quotes here will shock you, make you laugh, make you wonder . . .

1

Why We Hunt

You have to become a different person in the course of these years. For this is what the art of archery means: A profound and far-reaching contest of the archer with himself. You will see with other eyes and measure with other measures. It happens to all that are touched by the spirit of this art.

EUGEN HERRIGEL
ZEN IN THE ART OF ARCHERY (1948)

• • •

No one, but he who has partaken thereof, can understand
the keen delight of hunting in lonely lands. For him is
the joy of the horse well ridden and the rifle well held; for
the long days toil and hardship, resolutely endured, and
crowned at the end with triumph. In after years there shall
come forever to his mind the memory of endless prairies
shimmering in the bright sun, of vast snow-clad wastes of
lying desolate under grey skies; of the melancholy marshes;
of the rush of mighty rivers; of the breath of evergreen forest
in summer; of the crooning of ice-armored pines at the
touch of the winds in winter; of cataracts roaring between
hoary mountain masses; of all the innumerable sights and
sounds of the wilderness; of its immensity and mystery; and
of the silences that brood in its still depths.
THEODORE ROOSEVELT
THE WILDERNESS HUNTER (1891)

• • •

Pa did not like a country so old and worn out that the
hunting was poor. He wanted to go west. For two years he
had wanted to go west and take a homestead, but Ma did not
want to leave the settled country.
LAURA INGALLS WILDER (CIRCA 1900)

• • •

I heartily enjoy this life, with its perfect freedom, for I am very fond of hunting, and there are few sensations I prefer to that of galloping over these rolling limitless prairies, with rifle in hand, or winding my way among the barren, fantastic and grimly picturesque deserts of the so-called Bad Lands . . .
THEODORE ROOSEVELT
HUNTING TRIPS OF A RANCHMAN (1891)

• • •

There are no words that can tell the hidden spirit of the wilderness, that can reveal its mystery, its melancholy, and its charm.
THEODORE ROOSEVELT
HUNTING TRIPS OF A RANCHMAN (1885)

• • •

The farther one gets into the wilderness, the greater is the attraction of its lonely freedom."
THEODORE ROOSEVELT
HUNTING TRIPS OF A RANCHMAN (1885)

• • •

Old Flintlock, as friends and family knew [Archibald Rutledge], believed that hunting was the finest legacy a father could leave his offspring. It is my fixed conviction, he argued, that if a parent can give his children a passionate and wholesome devotion to the outdoors, the fact the he cannot leave each of them a fortune does not really matter. They will always enjoy life in its nobler aspects without money and without price.

JIM CASADA
SQUIRREL HUNTING: THE MAKING OF YOUNG HUNTERS (LATE 1990s)

• • •

One of the main advantages of hunting, my amiable readers, consists in its compelling you to be incessantly on the move from place to place, which is quite a pleasant thing for a man with nothing in particular to do.

IVAN TURGENEV
A HUNTER'S SKETCHES (1852)

• • •

In our rather stupid time, hunting is belittled and misunderstood, many refusing to see it for the vital vacation from the human condition that it is, or to acknowledge that the hunter does not hunt in order to kill; on the contrary, he kills in order to have hunted.
JOSÉ ORTEGA Y GASSET
MEDITATIONS ON HUNTING (1942)

• • •

I hunt to get in touch with an atavistic self that takes pure animal delight in the contest between hunter and hunted. In pheasant hunting I find my senses sharpened, my blood racing, and my whole being focused on what I am doing. I kill in order to have lived.
STEVE GROOMS
PHEASANT HUNTER'S HARVEST (1990)

• • •

. . . the finding and killing of the game is after all but a part of the whole.
THEODORE ROOSEVELT (CIRCA 1900)

• • •

On a hard hunting trip in mid-winter civilized man
learns once more
1. To earn his food and eat it with a hearty appetite;
2. To feel the delicious comfort of warmth and shelter
after extreme exposure;
3. To enjoy the life-renewing qualities of sound sleep
after utter exhaustion; and incidentally
4. To appreciate a respite from the eternal temptations
of sex.
J. WONG QUINCEY
CHINESE HUNTER (CIRCA 1938–39)

• • •

I wondered whether Kisik or any other great hunter could
ever tell which he really liked better, the hunting or the
eating. It was the old question in another form: Did he hunt
to eat or eat to hunt?
ANGUS CAMERON
"A HUNT WITH THE INNUIT" IN *SEASONS OF THE
HUNTER*
EDITED BY ELMAN AND SEYBOLD (1985)

• • •

September. It was, at last, September. If I shot him, it would be all over: the dawns to come and these twilights, the long, long walks through the country, the dead parsnip in the frosted meadows, and the musky smell of the bedded elk in the trampled grass. All over for another ten months . . . and all before I had watched and listened and smelled enough to be engaged with the season. I unloaded the rifle and closed the bolt.
TED KERASOTE
BLOODTIES (1993)

• • •

After more than 50 years of hunting, I'm pretty sure of two things: that hunting is too deeply rooted in the metaphysical to allow clinical examination, and that it's a happy man who keeps his youthful appetite for that sort of metaphysics.
JOHN MADSON
WHY MEN HUNT (1960)

• • •

What an absurd time to be a hunter. Yet has there ever been a more vital one?
THOMAS McINTYRE
"WHAT HUNTER KNOWS"
SPORTS AFIELD (1995)

• • •

Go to your freezer. How much and what kind of fish and game do you have left in there from the previous summer and fall getting freezer burn? Write it down and subtract it as penance from your bag limit this summer and fall.

JIM HARRISON
"A SPRING SERMON . . . OR SIBERIA"
SPORTS AFIELD (1994)

• • •

As far as enjoyment is concerned, I think that hunting is a lot more fun than killing, but, if you take away the ability to kill, you automatically take away most of the fun of hunting.

ERLE STANLEY GARDNER
HUNTING IS MORE FUN THAN KILLING (1949)

• • •

I hope you have an Old Duck Hunter in your life and I hope he lives in your blind . . . and shares your whiskey forever.

GENE HILL
"THE OLD DUCK HUNTER" IN *A HUNTER'S FIRESIDE BOOK* (1972)

• • •

Nature designed me as a meat-eating predator, and I accept
nature on its own terms, acknowledging death, including my
own (and yours, madam) as an essential aspect of life, not
to be euphemized or Disneyfied or otherwise denied. When
I kill a wild duck or pheasant cleanly and instantly, in the
fullness of its wild beauty and strong flight, I save the life of
a domestic duck or chicken, which would be killed in abject,
squawking terror.
When I kill a sharp-tailed grouse or bobwhite quail I become
part of the process of life, accepting and fulfilling my role
as predator and rejecting the destructive Old Testament
concept of man as something separate from nature.
ED ZERN
HUNTING AND FISHING FROM "A" TO ZERN (1985)

• • •

I believe hunters owe it to themselves to try to understand
what it is that urges them out. To fail to examine the source
of the hunting instinct is to fail to experience it fully.
CHARLES FERGUS
THE UPLAND EQUATION (1995)

• • •

. . . by hunting, man succeeds . . . in separating himself from
the present, and in renewing the primitive situations.
JOSÉ ORTEGA Y GASSET
MEDITATIONS ON HUNTING (1942)

• • •

Ten thousand years ago all men were hunters, including the
ancestors of everyone reading this book.
CARLETON S. COON
THE HUNTING PEOPLES (1971)

• • •

Another sharptail flew from the open hillside in the sunlight,
far too far away, and I thought, before I walked down into
the thorns, Gillis breathing beside me: At least they give
some illusion of choice. At least they give you that.
JOHN BARSNESS
WESTERN SKIES (1994)

• • •

2

The Essence of Hunting

Hunting with a dog and a gun is delightful in itself, but let us
suppose you were not born a hunter, but are fond of nature
and freedom all the same; you cannot then help envying us
hunters.

IVAN TURGENEV

A SPORTSMAN'S NOTEBOOK (1850)

• • •

The emotions that good hunters need to cultivate are love and service more than courage. The sentiments of the hunt then become translated into art.
JAMES SWAN
IN DEFENSE OF HUNTING (1995)

• • •

If a man undertakes a dangerous enterprise with determination to succeed or lose his life, he will do many things with ease and unharmed which a smaller degree of energy would not accomplish.
MESHACH BROWNING
FORTY-FOUR YEARS OF THE LIFE OF A HUNTER (1859)

• • •

The wildlife of today is not ours to do with what we please. The original stock was given to us in trust for the benefit both of the present and the future. We must render an accounting of this trust to those who come after us.
THEODORE ROOSEVELT (CIRCA 1900)

• • •

If there's a law about it at all, though who ever heard of a law, that a man shouldn't kill deer where he pleased!-but if there is a law at all, it should be to keep people from the use of smooth-bores. A body never knows where his lead will fly, when he pulls the trigger of one of them uncertain fire-arms.
JAMES FENIMORE COOPER
NATTY BUMPPO, IN *THE PIONEERS* (1823)

• • •

In wilderness is the preservation of the world.
HENRY DAVID THOREAU
"WALKING" (1854)

• • •

I have seen him set fire to his wigwam and smooth over the graves of his fathers . . . clap his hand in silence over his mouth, and take the last look over his fair hunting ground, and turn his face in sadness to the setting sun.
GEORGE CATLIN (EARLY 1800s)

• • •

If the only satisfaction to be derived from the sport lay
in killing birds, I would have quit the game long since.
BURTON SPILLER
MORE GROUSE FEATHERS (1938)

• • •

The hunter is the alert man.
JOSÉ ORTEGA Y GASSET
MEDITATIONS ON HUNTING (1942)

• • •

We reached the old wolf in time to watch a fierce green
fire dying in her eyes. I realized then, and have known ever
since, that there was something new to me in those eyes—
something known only to her and to the mountain. I was
young then, and full of trigger-itch; I thought that because
fewer wolves meant more deer, that no wolves would mean
hunters' paradise. But after seeing the green fire die, I sensed
that neither the wolf nor the mountain agreed with such a
view.
ALDO LEOPOLD
A SAND COUNTY ALMANAC (1949)

• • •

There is a passion for hunting something deeply implanted
in the human breast.
CHARLES DICKENS (CIRCA MID-1800s)

• • •

Why should I not be serious? I am speaking of hunting.
GENERAL ZAROFF
FROM "THE MOST DANGEROUS GAME"
BY RICHARD CONNELL (1924)

• • •

Like the predator he pursues, the wolf hunter is often as
reviled and hated as he is praised and honored. Many despise
him because he is killing a symbol of their idea of wilderness.
On the other hand, ranchers, hunters and victims hail him
as a hero, feed him dinner, and learn from him. This human
in wolf's clothing helps keep Nature's most efficient canine
predator in check.
CHRISTOPHER BATIN
WOLF HUNTER (1990s)

• • •

Have you looked over your shoulder lately? There is a beast
that lives in the rural forests, a beast that often watches
you without you knowing; perhaps as you fish a stream, or
maybe as you hunt birds in the local forest. This beast has
stalked and killed sportsmen, ambushing them when they
least expect it. And there's one out there now, waiting for
you, as you head out on your hunting trip with friends.
CHRISTOPHER BATIN
NIGHT OF THE BROWN BEAR (1990s)

• • •

Any autumn. Every autumn, so long as my luck holds and
my health, and if I win the race. The race is a long, slow one
that has been going on since I started to hunt again. The
race is between my real competence at hunting gradually
developing, and, gradually fading, the force of the fantasies
which have sustained me while the skills are still weak. If
the fantasies fade before the competence is really mine, I am
lost as a hunter because I cannot enjoy disgust. I will have to
stop, after all, and look for something else.
VANCE BOURJAILY
IN FIELDS NEAR HOME (1984)

• • •

The Daniel Boones among us notwithstanding—and I haven't met one yet—the average hunter pays his dues for every head of big game the same way that dues are exacted in other pursuits.
NORMAN STRUNG
HUNTING WITH LADY LUCK (EARLY 1990s)

• • •

If you happen to hunt a great deal, or if you spend a lot of time in the woods for any other reason, there always seems to be a half section of land, somewhere, that fits you better than it fits anybody else.
TOM KELLY
FORTY CROOK BRANCH (LATE 1990s)

• • •

We are measured more as hunters by the things we choose not to shoot, than by those that we do.
NORMAN STRUNG
THE MEASURE OF A HUNTER
FIELD & STREAM (1985)

• • •

If one were to present the sportsman with the death of the animal as a gift he would refuse it. What he is after is having to win it, to conquer the surly brute through his own effort and skill with all the extras that this carries with it: the immersion in the countryside, the healthfulness of the exercise, the distraction from his job.
JOSÉ ORTEGA Y GASSET
MEDITATIONS ON HUNTING (1942)

• • •

"Everybody," he said, "should be allowed to brag some about what he did good that day, and to cover up shameless on what he did wrong."
ROBERT RUARK
THE OLD MAN AND THE BOY (1953)

• • •

There is a code that you do not quit in the middle of a hunting trip. It may be a barbaric or juvenile expression of the stiff-upper-lip philosophy to go on when you do not want to, but it is the only thing you can do.
FRANK CALKINS
ROCKY MOUNTAIN WARDEN (1964)

• • •

He knew the troubles of tracking, The business of camps and kits, And the pleasure that pays For the pain of all, The ultimate shot that hits.
JAY MELLON
BREAKFAST AT MIDNIGHT
OUTDOOR LIFE (1969)

• • •

We cannot change the ultimate lives of the creatures we harbor in our world, but now and then by watching them we can gain some sense of what we are and just where we stand on the shelf . . . somewhere between the owls and the moles.
GENE HILL
"AN EVENING WALK" IN
A HUNTER'S FIRESIDE BOOK (1972)

• • •

We believe that we are instinctively born knowing the wilderness, that we are nowhere so comfortable as in the forest primeval, and that we are quite fully capable of hunting and killing with dispatch anything from hummingbirds to elephants, even if we choose not to do it. To admit ignorance . . . somehow runs against our grain.
TOM KELLY
TENTH LEGION (1973)

• • •

Of the reasons I go hunting again, the most irresistible,
whether or not it's much of an argument, is familial.
VANCE BOURJAILY
FOREWORD TO *SEASONS OF THE HUNTER*
EDITED BY ELMAN AND SEYBOLD (1985)

• • •

In order to discover the extremely cautious animal, he
resorted to the detective instinct of another animal; he asked
for its help.
JOSÉ ORTEGA Y GASSET
MEDITATIONS ON HUNTING (1942)

• • •

Man may have originated as a vegetarian, but he became
the fiercest predator of all, with the power to control all the
other animals and build the civilizations we have now.
LEE WULFF
TROUT ON A FLY (1986)

• • •

I like sporting guns because they are tools that help us fit into the natural puzzle; and fine sporting guns because they are wonderful objects.
STEPHEN BODIO
GOOD GUNS (1986)

• • •

Elation rules the camp when I bring in the deer. The scene could easily be from five thousand years ago, when the hungry people applaud the hunter as they realize that they aren't going to starve just yet.
JIM HAMM
BOWS & ARROWS OF THE NATIVE AMERICANS (1986)

• • •

At a minimum, a good gun must be useful, beautiful, and well-made enough to last a lifetime.
STEPHEN BODIO
GOOD GUNS (1986)

• • •

One last time before the season slips completely into the past, I want to listen to the silence and see again the stars reflected in the quiet water.
STEVEN MULAK
WAX AND WANE (1987)

• • •

I can't tell you what makes one man a hunter and another not. But I can tell you how this all happened for one hunter.
JIM FERGUS
A HUNTER'S ROAD (1992)

• • •

I am never in a hurry when I am hunting. If I am in a hurry I don't go hunting.
HAVILAH BABCOCK
"CALLING ON MY NEIGHBORS" IN
MY HEALTH IS BETTER IN NOVEMBER (1947)

• • •

For a place we visit only one week out of the year, we worry about it far too much.
RICK BASS
THE DEER PASTURE (1985)

• • •

As long as there is such a thing as a wild goose I leave them the meaning of freedom. As long as there is such a thing as a cock pheasant I leave them the meaning of beauty. As long as there is such a thing as a hunting dog I leave them the meaning of loyalty. As long as there is such a thing as a man's own gun and a place to walk free with it I leave them the feeling of responsibility. This is part of what I believe I have given them when I have given them their first gun.
GENE HILL
"THE FIRST GUN" IN *A HUNTER'S FIRESIDE BOOK*
(1972)

• • •

Predators kill for practice and want to be as good as they can be at the skills that keep them alive. Instinctively they know that some day life will be severe and the best of their breed, the ablest killers, will survive and the less capable will die.
LEE WULFF
TROUT ON A FLY (1986)

• • •

Old deer hunting friends are better than new ones. They took the test of time and passed. Old deer hunters are better than young ones. They know more and their hearts and legs make them move more slowly.

JAMES R. PIERCE
GUNS AND HUNTING (1993)

• • •

This youthful desire to go into the woods and build a camp away from one's home, to pass secrets and share intimately with one's friends while enjoying the changes of the season, must have been carried from childhood by some of these hunters. Returning annually has become a ritual, a re-creation of their childhood memories and experiences.

JOHN MILLER
DEER CAMP (1992)

• • •

If there is a sacred moment in the ethical pursuit of game, it is the moment you release the arrow or touch off the fatal shot.

JIM POSEWITZ
BEYOND FAIR CHASE (1994)

• • •

Once a hunter decides to shoot a gun or release an arrow,
there is no question of catch and release.
JAMES SWAN
IN DEFENSE OF HUNTING (1995)

• • •

By now the sun was halfway to noon, and as we worked
along a little creek bottom, a fallow field upslope flashed
what must have been a million cobwebs lacing each dried
weed. None was larger than a man's hand, and all were
backlit by the sun through melted frost in brilliant splendor.
It was as though Nature had sewn sequins on a gossamer
gown and dressed herself for a ball. I can still remember the
loveliness, and thinking how impermanent is beauty.
DAVID HENDERSON
SPOOK AND OTHER STORIES: TALES OF A BIRD DOG
(1995)

• • •

How do hunters know to hunt this field, this day? How do they know where to sink their pits? . . . It is not such a bad thing to feel, this anxiety. It is a kind of longing . . .
RICHARD FORD
"HUNTING WITH MY WIFE"
SPORTS AFIELD (1996)

• • •

You could tell how cold the morning was, despite the exertion, just by watching the steam roar from the [antelope's] abdominal cavity. I stuck the knife in the ground and sat back against the slope, looking clear across to Convict Grade and the Crazy Mountains. I was blood from the elbows down and the antelope's eyes had skinned over. I thought, this is goddamned serious and you had better always remember that.
THOMAS MCGUANE
THE HEART OF THE GAME (1990)

• • •

Oh how my heart will ever ache; when memory calls me back again; to crystal mountains, azure lakes, with eagles dancing in the wind.
BILLY ELLIS
HUNTER TO THE DAWN (1988)

• • •

When he finally came mincing through the trees all puffed up and blue in the face, the sun lit up his red wattles, and the copper and bronze lights in his body feathers were magnificent. I can still see his tail fanned full, turning this way and that in the early-morning sunlight as he sought the hen he had heard calling from where I sat.

JEROME B. ROBINSON
IN THE TURKEY WOODS (1998)

• • •

For [certain] men, the long wait until hunting season is like the long night before opening day. They are restless, tossing and turning and waiting for first light—or autumn. Their lives would be more placid and serene without hunting. But then, the churchyards are filled with serene, placid men who did not hunt.

JOHN MADSON
GOING OUT MORE (1974)

• • •

It boils down to this: Accept your hunting partners like your mate—for better or worse.
JOEL VANCE
BOBS, BRUSH, AND BRITTANIES: A LONG LOVE AFFAIR WITH QUAIL HUNTING (1997)

• • •

What, after the fat is boiled away, is the essence of hunting dangerous game? In a word, it is challenge in its most elemental form, the same challenge that provided the drive that brought the hairless, puny-toothed, weak, dawn-creature that became man down out of the trees to hunt meat with his rocks, clubs and pointed sticks. This daring still lives, in various degrees of mufti, under the flannel breast of the meekest shoe clerk . . .
PETER HATHAWAY CAPSTICK
DEATH IN THE LONG GRASS (1977)

• • •

We kill the game to eat it. Tasting it, we thank it. Thanking it, we remember it: how we hunted it, how it tested us, how we overcame it, how it finally fell.
CHARLES FERGUS
A ROUGH-SHOOTING DOG (1991)

• • •

She squeezed the trigger and saw the eye explode, the dark
bulk fall, the dream enact and love and blood meld into
a stream, in the solitude, the hunter's solitude, and she
murmured, "I am so terribly goddamned sorry," and cried
again against the walnut stock of the rifle in the silence.
JACK CURTIS
DAWN WATERS (1998)

• • •

I don't regard nature as a spectator sport.
ED ZERN
HUNTING AND FISHING FROM "A" TO ZERN (1985)

• • •

The best part of hunting and fishing was the thinking about
going and the talking about it after you got back.
ROBERT RUARK
THE OLD MAN AND THE BOY (1953)

• • •

. . . the boy's arrogance was quickly dispelled by the next step of his induction into the fraternity of hunters. Gutting is, ordinarily, the responsibility of the man who shot the deer. This time, Russ did the honors (as do many uncles) of instructing the boy.
JOHN MILLER
DEER CAMP (1992)

• • •

I've got eleven months to go—before it's mid-November and bitter cold, And the sun is rising and I am growing old . . .
PETER J. FIDUCCIA
WHITETAIL STRATEGIES (1995)

• • •

Despite his many faults in the field, I'm grateful to him in a way. Now I know what to avoid when somebody new asks me to go hunting with him.
ROBERT F. JONES
DANCERS IN THE SUNSET SKY (1996)

• • •

Humans are not inherently violent creatures. We are predators, but predation exists within the natural order while violence exists beyond it. Loud violence estranges us, and quiet violence is the state from which we've been estranged.
ALLEN JONES
A QUIET PLACE OF VIOLENCE (1997)

• • •

Here was a boy of depth, character and awareness. A bowhunter. An athlete blessed by God, and I, a father, blessed with him.
TED NUGENT
IN *SPORTS AFIELD* (1997)

• • •

The wilderness reminded him that everything he did had a consequence.
STEPHEN BODIO
ON THE EDGE OF THE WILD (1998)

• • •

3

Afield

The hunter, like the savage whose place he filled, seemed
to select among the blind signs of their wild route with a
species of instinct, seldom abating his speed, and never
pausing to deliberate.
JAMES FENIMORE COOPER
THE LAST OF THE MOHICANS (1826)

• • •

You need to be familiar with the field, the woods, the marsh, the forest, or the mountains where you hunt. If you work hard and long at this aspect of hunting, you can become a part of the place you hunt. You will sense when you start to belong to the country.

JIM POSEWITZ

BEYOND FAIR CHASE (1994)

• • •

I finally managed to reach the end of the woods, but there was no road of any sort there: some kind of untouched low bushes spread far and wide before me, while beyond them, ever so far, one could glimpse a desertlike field. I stopped again. "What is all this! Come, where am I?"

IVAN TURGENEV

THE HUNTING SKETCHES (1852)

• • •

The dog was disappointed and yearned back towards the fire. This man did not know cold. Possibly all the generations of his ancestry had been ignorant of cold, of real cold, of cold one hundred and seven degrees below the freezing point. But the dog knew; all its ancestry knew, and it had inherited the knowledge. And it knew that it was not good to walk abroad in such fearful cold.

JACK LONDON
"TO BUILD A FIRE" (CIRCA 1900)
IN *THE UNABRIDGED JACK LONDON* (1981)

• • •

Some people can do better with one rifle and some with another, and in the long run it is "the man behind the gun" that counts most.

THEODORE ROOSEVELT
"HUNTING IN THE CATTLE COUNTRY" IN H*UNTING
IN MANY LANDS*
EDITED BY ROOSEVELT AND GRINNELL (1895)

• • •

He is not an educated man, but . . . is never lost . . . he adds
the singularly retentive memory of peculiarities and of every
incident in his own history and that of his companions
. . . Everything Bridger has seen, he recollects with entire
precision, and in his wild life . . . he has traversed the whole
country in many directions.

J. CECIL ALTER
JIM BRIDGER (1979)

• • •

Come face to face with a brownie at close range, near enough
to hear the low rumbling in his chest, and no other wild
animal noise will ever scare you again.

BEN EAST
OUTDOOR LIFE (1945)

• • •

That night around my fire I heard howling far to the west of
me, perhaps several miles away. Sure as God a wolf.

JIM HARRISON
WOLF: A FALSE MEMOIR (1989)

• • •

I like to hope that somehow he survived, to live out his days
in some distant range, and I almost wish that I had never
seen him alive at all. It's a fearful thing to know that the wild
held something so splendid, and that you spoiled it.
JOHN S. MARTIN
OUTDOORS LIMITED (1947)

• • •

"Well," I thought, "here is the situation which you have
visualized for more than ten years. You know what to do.
Don't wait any longer. If it is necessary to spend a night
in the woods, spend it as comfortably as possible. Make
camp-and make it now."
LAWRENCE R. KOLLER
SHOTS AT WHITETAILS (1948)

• • •

When I heard the full-throated bawling howl, I should have
had chills racing up and down my spine. Instead, I was
thrilled to know that the big grays might have picked up
my trail and were following me down the glistening frozen
highway of the river.
SIGURD OLSON
THE SINGING WILDERNESS (1956)

• • •

God doesn't count the hours you spend afield with friends.
GENE HILL
"THE PRIMROSE PATH" IN *A HUNTER'S FIRESIDE
BOOK* (1972)

• • •

The first track is the end of the string. At the far end, a being
is moving; a mystery, dropping a hint about itself every so
many feet, telling you more about itself until you can almost
see it, even before you come to it.
TOM BROWN
THE TRACKER (1978)

• • •

"Pshaw!" muttered Abiram; "the boy, has killed a buck, or,
perhaps a buffaloe, and he is sleeping by the carcass to keep
off the wolves 'till day; we shall soon see him, or hear him,
bawling for help to bring in his load."
JAMES FENIMORE COOPER
THE LAST OF THE MOHICANS (1826)

• • •

My first sight was a kitchen match held to the bow with a
rubber band.
FRED BEAR
FRED BEAR'S WORLD OF ARCHERY (1979)

• • •

I admit that the game of deer-hunting is sometimes tedious
and the shooting of the occasional variety; yet my experience
has been that the great chance does come to the faithful, and
that to make good on it is to drink one of Life's rarest juleps,
the memory of whose flavor is a delight for years.
ARCHIBALD RUTLEDGE
"PLANTATION GAME TRAILS" IN
THE DEER BOOK BY LAMAR UNDERWOOD (1980)

• • •

The heart of [this] hunter looks for a piece of Eden. It feels
right to hunt in a place where the land is healthy.
GEORGE N. WALLACE
HIGH COUNTRY NEWS (1983)

• • •

Probably few of my readers have had occasion to drop in at
village taverns—but as to us hunters, where won't we go!
IVAN TURGENEV
THE HUNTING SKETCHES (1852)

• • •

The Iroquois Confederation called the Adirondacks" the
dark and bloody land," too wild to civilize and suitable
only for warfare, hunting, and little else. Since that time,
twentieth-century technology and population booms have
made few inroads.
A. J. MCCLANE
*GREAT FISHING AND HUNTING LODGES OF NORTH
AMERICA* (1984)

• • •

For hunting, .22s are mainly useful on squirrels. You cannot
kill either a turkey or a woodchuck consistently with
a .22 . . .
STEPHEN BODIO
GOOD GUNS (1986)

• • •

I had my rifle turned around and ready by the time it was gone. I had figured elk, because that's all I had seen. The word moose was just working its way forward in my mind when I saw it sidehilling along the opposite bluff . . .
PETE FROMM
INDIAN CREEK CHRONICLES (1993)

• • •

It is regrettable that of the hundreds of thousands of deer hunters spread throughout our whitetail deer country only a few spend sufficient time in the woods for absorbing some knowledge of deer habits.
LAWRENCE R. KOLLER
SHOTS AT WHITETAILS (1948)

• • •

If once I could blame a failed duck hunt on boyish restlessness or bungling, now I can generally blame the simple absence of game. I've become a better retriever trainer, a better duck caller and a better shot over the years—years that locally reduce these skills to near irrelevance. Too soon old, too late smart, as they say.
SYDNEY LEA
HUNTING THE WHOLE WAY HOME (1994)

• • •

You have to wonder what goes through a dog's mind. There are those who say, Not much, but I'm not one of them.
DAN O'BRIEN
EQUINOX: LIFE, LOVE, AND BIRDS OF PREY (1997)

• • •

4

Etcetera

I kill it, I grill it . . .
TED NUGENT
KILL IT & GRILL IT (2002)

• • •

All animals will not only be not shot, they will be
protected—not only from people but as much as possible
from each other. Prey will be separated from predator, and
there will be no overpopulation or starvation because all will
be controlled by sterilization or implant.
CLEVELAND AMORY,
FOUNDER OF THE FUND FOR ANIMALS
DESCRIBING HIS IDEAL WORLD, IN SIERRA, (JUNE 1992)

• • •

Hunting, fishing, drawing, and music occupied my every moment. Cares I knew not, and cared naught about them
JOHN JAMES AUDUBON (EARLY 1800s)

• • •

They might in the future more than ever before engage in hunting beavers.
SAMUEL DE CHAMPLAIN (CIRCA 1600)

• • •

. . . wild flowers should be enjoyed unplucked where they grow.
THEODORE ROOSEVELT
HUNTING TRIPS OF A RANCHMAN (1885)

• • •

I am happy now, to recall that I was not only his son but his companion, and whenever there was a hunting expedition or any other pleasure, I was always with him.
JOHN PHILIP SOUSA (CIRCA 1900)

• • •

When he was young, I told Dale Jr. that hunting and racing are a lot alike. Holding that steering wheel and holding that rifle both mean you better be responsible.
DALE EARNHARDT (LATE 1990S)

• • •

One day you get no chances for all your struggle. Or, worse yet, you fail chances that you should have seized. Another time you make them all. If you consistently get limits, however, consider making the rules more difficult for yourself. Field sports are not about targets and scores. Score-keeping is necessary in competitions between humans, unattractive in competitions with weaker adversaries. Consistent scores of many to zero do not smell of struggle and chance. They smell of greed.
DATUS PROPER
STRUGGLE AND CHANCE: WHY WE DO IT (1991)

• • •

There are few things most outdoor-minded men pride themselves on more than the ability to build a good fire.
GENE HILL
LOG FIRES (1967)

• • •

There is no reason why, with proper care and enforcement of necessary restrictions, the Jackson's Hole [Wyoming] district may not be kept as a game paradise, where sportsmen may come from all parts of the world and kill game, thus bringing to the state hundreds of thousands of dollars annually, at the same time preventing the utter extinction of animals that are indigenous to the country and of increasing interest.
OUTDOOR LIFE (1899)

• • •

I know of no more common fault among parents. No matter how zealously guarded a boy's life may be, the time will almost certainly come when he will either handle firearms, or find himself in the company of other boys who are doing so, and in either case his chance of emerging from the affair in a watertight condition is in direct proportion to the familiarity the participants have with the weapon.
BURTON SPILLER
MORE GROUSE FEATHERS (1938)

• • •

Hunters and the government have different objectives. Most hunters want to see as many waterfowl as possible and be able to shoot a few. In contrast, the U.S. Fish and Wildlife Service tries to manage ducks so that hunters can kill all they see.
GEORGE REIGER
HERON HILL CHRONICLE (1994)

• • •

Man is a fugitive from nature.
JOSÉ ORTEGA Y GASSET
MEDITATIONS ON HUNTING (1942)

• • •

I have always observed that the sportsmen who really know invariably hang their game in a natural position: that is, by the head.
ARCHIBALD RUTLEDGE
IN *SHOTGUNNING IN THE LOWLANDS* BY RAY P. HOLLAND (1945)

• • •

The truth is, most guides are not smart enough to hold down
a steady job at the local sawmill, and are obliged to choose
between guiding and burglary.
ED ZERN
TO HELL WITH HUNTING (1946)

• • •

One evening after I had turned in, the flap of my tent opened
and the [French] countess came in wearing a lace Parisian
nightgown that covered her but poorly and carrying a beer
glass full of whiskey. She sat down on the edge of my cot,
offered me a drink, and then took one herself. "Hunter, my
friend, I am lonely," she told me sadly. "Countess, where's
your husband?" I asked her. She looked at me a long time.
"Hunter, you Englishmen ask the strangest questions," she
said and flounced out of my tent.
JOHN A. HUNTER
HUNTER (1952)

• • •

We still do not realize that today we can enjoy the wilderness without fear, do not appreciate the part that predators play in the balanced ecology of any natural community. We seem to prefer herds of semi-domesticated deer and elk and moose, swarms of small game with their natural alertness gone.

SIGURD OLSON
THE SINGING WILDERNESS (1956)

• • •

. . . she was prone to claim she was so dreadfully bored by suitors—all of whom seemed limited in their sphere of interests to business, hunting, and horses—that she felt she ought to have a sign fashioned to read Gentlemen Prohibited hanging from the porch gate.

CHARLES FRAZIER
COLD MOUNTAIN (1997)

• • •

Robin Hood and his merry men would envy the modern-day bowhunter.

FRED BEAR
FRED BEAR'S WORLD OF ARCHERY (1979)

• • •

I hope you are shot in the gut and lie in a cold wet ditch and die slowly.
A LETTER TO ED ZERN, IN RESPONSE TO A BIRD-HUNTING
ARTICLE HE HAD WRITTEN, QUOTED IN
HUNTING AND FISHING FROM "A" TO ZERN (1985)

• • •

A new subspecies of human, the animals rights activists, has suddenly appeared, and they have a large following.
JAMES SWAN
IN DEFENSE OF HUNTING (1995)

• • •

I have known many meat eaters to be far more non-violent than vegetarians.
MAHATMA GANDHI
IN *GANDHI ON NONVIOLENCE* BY THOMAS MERTON
(1964)

• • •

The man who said "The only experience a man can't recover
from is hanging," is wrong. He never tried to raise three
Labrador puppies.
GENE HILL
"RAISING PUPPIES, PART II" IN *A HUNTER'S FIRESIDE
BOOK* (1972)

• • •

Once he opens his mouth, there is no doubting. The
conversation of an Outdoorsman is as different from that of
Others as a solunar table is from the breakfast table.
RICK BASS
THE DEER PASTURE (1985)

• • •

I'm not sure where in my anatomy the hunting impulse
resides—in my genes, some would say, or in my soul but it's
certainly there as, I'm convinced, it is in all of us.
WILLIAM G. TAPPLY
SPORTSMAN'S LEGACY (1993)

• • •

The wilderness thrills us and gives us life, and while
we nurture the traditions of our grandfathers and
grandmothers, we are saddened by what we anticipate for
our grandchildren. Sometimes, sitting silently in the forest
or climbing into the mountains, it occurs to us that we do
not want to go home because we have begun to think of
ourselves as an endangered species. To hell with that.
TERRY McDONELL
"WHO WE ARE" IN *THE BEST OF SPORTS AFIELD* BY
JAY CASSELL (1996)

• • •

We all have our days when the gun barrel is crooked and
the game has the last laugh. If we complain about our lot in
the matter of game and hunting, that's probably one of the
things that we have in common with our ancestors.
RON FORSYTH
REFLECTIONS, MAN AND BOY (1997)

• • •

What this country really needs, I decided, is a good cheap
chigger remedy.
HAVILAH BABCOCK
"HOW TO GET RID OF CHIGGERS" IN *MY HEALTH IS
BETTER IN NOVEMBER* (1947)

• • •

In these delicate times, people who actually deal with fish,
birds or mammals before all edible parts are wrapped in
plastic are looked on either as half-wits . . . or barbarians.
JOHN BARSNESS
WESTERN SKIES (1994)

• • •

I see no reason to apologize for being a hunter, particularly
in this age. What comparable sweetness, mystery, and
wonder can be found in the Styrofoam-dished, Saran-
wrapped, boneless, skinless chicken breasts at the meat
counter of the supermarket?
JIM FERGUS
A HUNTER'S ROAD (1992)

• • •

Rikki-tikki had a right to be proud of himself; but he did not grow too proud, and he kept that garden as a mongoose should keep it, with tooth and jump and spring and bite, till never a cobra dared show its head inside the walls.

RUDYARD KIPLING
"RIKKI-TIKKI-TAVI" IN *THE JUNGLE BOOKS* (1894)

• • •

A warden's time is spent counting, recounting, and then re-recounting some wild population, or the ratio of their sexes, or even (as with the pellets) their signs.

FRANK CALKINS
ROCKY MOUNTAIN WARDEN (1964)

• • •

I think it was Jim Harrison who said that, in a debate between the NRA and proponents of gun control, he'd rather be in a rowboat. Although I am a longtime member of the NRA, I know what he means; I can think of nothing more mind-deadening than being in the presence of two debaters with their minds made up, who reiterate the same old arguments at the top of their voices while utterly ignoring or missing each other's points.

STEPHEN BODIO
ON THE EDGE OF THE WILD (1998)

• • •

Around here turkey shoots are as common as 'possums.
JIM CARMICHEL
JUST JIM (1969)

• • •

Hunting is one of the hardest things even to think about.
Such a storm of conflicting emotions!
EDWARD ABBEY
ONE LIFE AT A TIME, PLEASE (1988)

• • •

How can any man or woman, city born and bred, expect
to know firsthand—to understand—that killing is a daily
part of life for all of us. They know, of course. But a lack of
thoughtful interest, even outright denial, is easier without
any personal involvement.
M. R. JAMES
MY PLACE (1992)

• • •

It's important to believe that you've spent enough time there, watching, listening, intermingling; and to know that what you're doing—killing—is not only imperfect and unclear, but can also be done respectfully only when you remain unsure and somewhat doubtful.
TED KERASOTE
HEART OF HOME (1993)

• • •

I ran a trapline that taught me more about nature than anything else I've ever done.
GEORGE REIGER
HERON HILL CHRONICLE (1994)

• • •

To keep our opportunity to hunt, we must always remember that wildlife belongs to all the people. The future of hunting depends upon how the majority of people view hunters. These people form their opinions when they see how we hunt and how we care for, and about, wildlife.
JIM POSEWITZ
BEYOND FAIR CHASE (1994)

• • •

Suzie doesn't approve of hunting in any form. "That's what cattle are for," she said.
RICK BASS
IN THE LOYAL MOUNTAINS (1995)

• • •

Like most Americans, I had no experience with any kind of hunting, knew essentially nothing about it, and couldn't fathom why anyone would want to kill and eat a wild animal.
RICHARD K. NELSON
FINDING COMMON GROUND (1996)

• • •

[Dogs] have a much stronger bond to humans than any other species, stronger than horses, or cats, or even falcons . . . After all, they are the only animal to have volunteered for domestication.
DAN O'BRIEN
EQUINOX; LIFE, LOVE, AND BIRDS OF PREY (1997)

• • •

A strange new animal stalks the woods in North America: the eco-redneck. *Ecce homo.* It is an obvious irony to some, an unintentional one to others, but these days sporting persons and environmentalists are apt to be one and the same.
STEVE CHAPPLE
CONFESSIONS OF AN ECO-REDNECK (1997)

• • •

I believe that animals—birds and animals, anyway—do think, but that they think in ways that would seem alien and frightening to us if we could inhabit their minds.
STEPHEN BODIO
ON THE EDGE OF THE WILD (1998)

• • •

What a dreary, monolithic suburban culture we shall be, when all eccentric passions have been stamped out.
MAX HASTINGS, ON THE LABOR PARTY'S EFFORTS TO BAN FOX HUNTING AND OTHER BLOOD SPORTS IN BRITAIN
THE FIELD (APRIL 1997)

• • •

There can be no excuse for losing a buck from which blood
has been drawn . . . In my camp, the failure to find a buck
known to be wounded is a distinct stigma, keenly felt by all
of us.
JOHN WOOTTERS
HUNTING TROPHY DEER (1997)

• • •

We, as hunters, are increasingly going to find ourselves
in circumstances where we must define and defend our
position. The possession of firearms is a right, but hunting
is a privilege. Anti-hunters are fanatics for sure, but they are
well funded and well represented. We need to be smarter
these days. We need to be more respectful toward the game
we hunt.
MIKE GOULD
THE LABRADOR SHOOTING DOG (1998)

• • •

Works and Authors Quoted

Edward Abbey
    One Life at a Time, Please (1988)

Abenaki hunter (undated)

Cecil J. Alter
    Jim Bridger (1979)

Russell Annabel
    "Now You Take Bear" (1943)
    Speaking of Sheep Hunting: Tales of A Big Game Guide (1938)

Antler
    Factory (1980)

Havilah Babcock
    My Health is Better in November (1947)

John Barsness
Western Skies (1994)

Rick Bass
In The Loyal Mountains (1995)
The Deer Pasture (1985)

Fred Bear
Fred Bear's World of Archery (1979)

Peter Beard and Alistair Graham
Eyelids of Morning (1974)

W.D.M. "Karamojo" Bell
On Rifles and Shooting (1950)

Stephen Bodio
Good Guns (1986)
On the Edge of the Wild (1998)

Vance Bourjaily
Foreword to *Seasons of the Hunter* edited by
Elman and Seybold (1985)

Paul Brandreth
Trails of Enchantment (1930)

Tom Brown
The Tracker (1978)

Charles L. Cadieux
Goose Hunting (1979)

Frank Calkins
Rocky Mountain Warden (1964)

Angus Cameron
"A Hunt with the Innuit" in *Seasons of the Hunter*
Edited by Elman and Seybold

Peter Hathaway Capstick
Death in the Long Grass (1977)

Jim Carmichel
Just Jim (1969)

Jay Cassell
"The Rack" (1992)

John Dean Caton
The Antelope and Deer of North America (1877)

Steve Chapple
Confessions of an Eco-Redneck (1997)

Carleton S. Coon
The Hunting Peoples (1971)

James Fenimore Cooper
The Last of the Mohicans
Natty Bumpo, in *The Deerslayer* (1842)

Natty Bumppo, in The Pioneers
Jim Corbett Man-Eaters of Kumaon (1946)

Jack Curtis
Dawn Waters (1998)
Comte Alfred D'Orsay (1850)

Billy Ellis
Hunter to the Dawn (1988)

George Bird Evans
An Affair with Grouse (1982)

William Faulkner
"The Bear" (1931)
Big Woods (1955)

Charles Fergus
A Rough-Shooting Dog (1991)
The Upland Equation (1995)

Jim Fergus
A Hunter's Road (1992)

Peter J. Fiduccia
Whitetail Strategies (1995)

Corey Ford
*The Road to Tinkhamtow*n (1970)

Richard Ford
"Hunting with My Wife" (1996)

Frank Forrester (1807-1858)

Ron Forsyth
Reflections, Man and Boy (1997)

William Harnden Foster
New England Grouse Shooting (1947)

Charles Frazier
Cold Mountain (1997)

Pete Fromm
Indian Creek Chronicles (1993)

Mahatma Gandhi
  In Gandhi on Nonviolence, by Thomas Merton (1964)

Erle Stanley Gardner
  Hunting Is More Fun than Killing (1964)

Mike Gould
  The Labrador Shooting Dog (1998)
  Gray's Sporting Journal (October 1990)

George Bird Grinnell (1879)

Steve Grooms
  Pheasant Hunter's Harvest (1990)

H. Rider Haggard
  Autobiography (1925)

Jim Hamm
  Bows & Arrows of the Native Americans (1986)

Michael Hanback
  Spring Gobbler Fever (1996)

Robert Hardy
  Longbow: A Social and Military History (1976)

Jim Harrison
  "A Spring Sermon . . . Or Siberia" (1994)
  Wolf: A False Memoir (1989)

Max Hastings
  In the Field (April 1997)

Ernest Hemingway
> *A Farewell to Arms* (1929)
> *Green Hills of Africa* (1935)

David Henderson
> *Spook and Other Stories: Tales of a Bird Dog* (1995)

Gene Hill
> *A Hunter's Fireside Book* (1972)

Ray P. Holland
> *Shotgunning in the Lowlands* (1945)

Pam Houston
> *Cowboys Are My Weakness* (1991)

John A. Hunter
> In *Safari: A Chronicle of Adventure*, by Bartle Bull (1988)
> *Hunter* (1952)

M. R. James
> *My Place* (1992)

Allen Jones
> *A Quiet Place of Violence* (1997)

Robert F. Jones
> *Dancers in the Sunset Sky* (1996)
> *It Wouldn't Be the Same* (1996)
> Keewatin Eskimo saying (undated)

Elmer Keith
> *Africa's Big Fire* (1960)
> *Big Game Hunting* (1948)

Tom Kelly
Tenth Legion (1973)
Better on a Rising Tide (1995)

Horace Kephart
Camping and Woodcraft (1917)
Our Southern Highlanders (1917)

Ted Kerasote
Bloodties (1993)
Heart of Home (1993)

James Kilgo
Deep Enough for Ivoryhills (1988)

Rudyard Kipling
The Jungle Books (1894)

Lawrence R. Koller
Shots at Whitetails (1948)

Sydney Lea
Hunting the Whole Way Home (1994)

Aldo Leopold
A Sand County Almanac (1949)
Red Legs Kicking (1946)

Meriwether Lewis (1805)

Meriwether Lewis and William Clark
The Journals of Lewis and Clark (1804)

Jack London
"To Build a Fire" (circa 1900) in *The Unabridged Jack London* (1981)

Dr. W. Brandon Macomber
"A Double Lion Mauling," in *African Hunter* by James Mellon (1975)

Gordon MacQuarrie
Stories of the Old Duck Hunters & Other Drivel (1967)

John Madson
Going Out More (1974)
"Why Men Hunt" (1960s)

David Mamet
"Deer Hunting" (1994)

John S. Martin
Outdoors Limited (1947)

Cormac McCarthy
The Crossing (1994)

A. J. McClane
Great Fishing and Hunting Lodges of North America (1984)

H. McCracken and H. van Cleve
Trapping: The Craft and Science of Catching Fur-Bearing Animals (1947)

Terry McDonell
"Who We Are" in The Best of Sports Afield by Jay Cassell (1996)

Thomas McGuane
"The Heart of the Game" (1990)

Thomas McIntyre
Dreaming the Lion (1993)
The Way of the Hunter (1988)
"What the Hunter Knows" (1995)

Joe Meeks
In *Great Hunting and Fishing Lodges of North America* by
A. J. McClane (1984)

James Mellon
African Hunter (1975)

Jay Mellon
"Breakfast at Midnight" (1969)

James A. Michener
Chesapeake (1978)

Edna St. Vincent Millay
"The Return" (1934)

John Miller
Deer Camp (1992)

John Mitchell
The Hunt (1979)

Thomas Morton
New English Canaan (1637)

Steven Mulak
Wax and Wane (1987)

John Myers Myers
The Wild Yazoo (1947)

Richard K. Nelson
Finding Common Ground (1996)

Geoffrey Norman
The Orvis Book of Upland Bird Shooting (1985)

Northwest Coast Indian song (undated)

Ted Nugent (1997)

Dan O'Brian
Equinox: Life, Love, and Birds of Prey (1997)

Harrison O'Connor
The Art of Hunting Big Game in North America (1967)

Annie Oakley
"Annie Oakley Ruled the Traps" (August 1915)

Sigurd Olson
"Shift of the Wind" (1944)
The Singing Wilderness (1956)

Clyde Ormond
Hunting Our Biggest Game (1956)
The Complete Book of Hunting (1962)

José Ortega y Gasset
Meditations on Hunting (1942)
Outdoor Life (1899)

John Ozoga
Whitetail Country (1992)

Alfred Pease
Book of the Lion (1987)

B.R. "Buck" Peterson
The Compleat Waterfo(u)wler (1996)

James R. Pierce
Guns and Hunting (1993)

Marco Polo (thirteenth century)

Dr. Saxon Pope
Hunting with the Bow and Arrow (1923)

Jim Posewitz
Beyond Fair Chase (1994)

Chaim Potok
I Am the Clay (1992)

Edgar M. Queeny
Prairie Wings (1946)

J. Wong Quincey
Chinese Hunter (circa 1938-39)

Austin L. Rand
American Water and Game Birds (1956)

John Randolph
"Hawk Who Walks Hunting" in *Seasons of the Hunter* by
Elman and Seybold (1985)

George Reiger
Heron Hill Chronicle (1994)
Wildfowler's Season (1995)
The Wildfowler's Quest (1989)

Jerome B. Robinson
In the Turkey Woods (1998)

Jimmy Robinson
Rockets of the North (1937)

Theodore Roosevelt
"Hunting in the Cattle Country" in *Hunting in Many Lands*, edited by Roosevelt and Grinnell (1895)
Outdoor Pastimes of an American Hunter (1905)
The Deer Family (1902)

Robert Ruark
Horn of the Hunter (1954)
The Old Man and the Boy (1953)
Use Enough Gun (1952)

Jonathan Ruffer
The Big Shots—Edwardian Shooting Parties (1977)

Eric Rundgren
"My First Leopard Mauling" in *African Hunter* by James Mellon (1975)

Archibald Rutledge
"Plantation Game Trails" in *The Deer Book* by Lamar Underwood (1980)
Days Off in Dixie (1924)
Why I Taught My Boys to Hunt (early 1940s)

Ernest Seton-Thompson
Lives of the Hunted (1901)
Lives of Game Animals (1929)

Sioux buffalo chant (undated)

Steve Smith
Hunting Ducks and Geese (1984)

"Song of the Elk," according to the Sioux Elk Society in *Dog Soldiers, Bear Men and Buffalo Women* by Thomas E. Mails

Burton Spiller
More Grouse Feathers (1938)

Curtis Stadtfeld
Whitetail Deer (1975)

Gen. William E. Strong
A Trip to Indian Territory with General P. H. Sheridan (Late 1800s)

Mark Sullivan
The Purification Ceremony (1997)

Daisetz T. Suzuki
Zen and the Art of Archery, translated by Eugen Herrigel (1964)

James Swan
In Defense of Hunting (1995)

William G. Tapply
Sportsman's Legacy (1993)

Bill Tarrant (1983)

E. Donnall Thomas
To All Things a Season (1997)

Henry David Thoreau
Walden (1854)
"Walking" (1854)

Leo Tolstoy
Anna Karenina (1877)
War and Peace (1969)

Ivan Turgenev
A Hunter's Sketches (1852)
A Sportsman's Notebook (1850)
The Hunting Sketches (1852)

Lamar Underwood
On Dangerous Grounds (1989)

Guy de la Valdene
For a Handful of Feathers (1995)

Joel Vance
Bobs, Brush, and Brittanies: A Long Love Affair with Quail Hunting (1997)

George N. Wallace
High Country News (1983)

"Bigfoot" Wallace
The Adventures of Bigfoot Wallace (1966)

Lord Warwick in Jonathan Ruffer's *The Big Shots—Edwardian Shooting Parties* (1985)

Col. Townsend Whelen
Mr. Rifleman (with Bradford Angier) (1965)

Casper W. Whitney
"The Cougar" in *Hunting in Many Lands* edited by Roosevelt and Grinnell (1895)

Roger D. Williams
"Wolf-Coursing" in *Hunting in Many Lands* edited by Roosevelt and Grinnell (1895)

Craig Woods
"The Endless Cover" in *Seasons of the Hunter* by Elman and Seybold (1985)

John Wootters
Hunting Trophy Deer (1997)

Albert Hazen Wright
Early Records of the Wild Turkey (1914)

Lee Wulff
Trout on a Fly (1986)

Dudley Young
Origin of the Sacred (1991)

Ed Zern
Hunting and Fishing from "A" to Zern (1985)
To Hell with Hunting (1946)

Notes on Selected Authors

Following are thoughts and observations about some of the many authors in this book. Some are friends and/or acquaintances, past and present; some are authors who we've admired from afar.

Russell Annabel. His stories of the wild and woolly days of frontier Alaska are part of our outdoor lore. Jay has spent time fishing in the Talkeetna Mountains, where "Rusty" did much of his hunting. They seem to be about as wild now as they were then.

John Barsness. Lives in a remote part of Montana and is one of the true bards of the West.

Rick Bass. Rick Bass, who lives in the Yaak Valley of northern Montana, has written numerous magazine articles and prize-winning books. His most recent book was *The Lost Grizzlies*:

A Search for Survivors in the Wilderness of Colorado. Our personal favorite has always been *The Deer Pasture.*

Fred Bear. The undisputed father of modern bowhunting.

Peter Beard. Peter Beard's photography is exceptional, his work in Africa unparalleled

Walter Dalrymple Maitland "Karamojo" Bell. Bell is the first hunter to ever take a high-powered rifle to East Africa. A professional elephant hunter and artist-adventurer, his books on hunting are must-reads.

Stephen Bodio. Stephen J. Bodio is a full-time writer, and old-fashioned naturalist, and a true sportsman. His book reviews are world famous.

Vance Bourjaily. Vance Bourjaily wrote for many magazines over the years, including *The New Yorker* and *Esquire.* Probably his best known book is *The Unnatural Enemy.*

Paul Brandreth. Naturalist, conservationist, and buckskin-clad hunter from the Adirondacks, Paulina Brandreth used "Paul" for fear she would not be taken seriously in a male-dominated sport. Her book *Trains of Enchantment* (1930) is a classic.

Tom Brown. Tom runs a wilderness survival school in New Jersey, with a spreading network of similar institutions throughout the country, and knows the ways of the natural world as well as anyone. He's been trying for years to get Kay to attend his school; he may yet.

Frank Calkins. Frank Calkins was a game warden in Utah who protected game animals, pursued lawbreakers, helped law abiders—and never forgot that he too was once a small boy with a rod and a gun.

Peter Hathaway Capstick. Long known as the great white hunter of the twentieth century, Capstick wrote of his experiences in compelling fashion. He has many followers, many skeptics,

Jim Carmichel. The longtime shooting editor of *Outdoor Life*, Jim Carmichel is one of the most respected names in the field today. He taught Jay's wife, Lorrain, how to shoot and shoot well—something Jay will always hold against him.

James Fenimore Cooper. Cooper's Leatherstocking Tales give the reader a close look at New York in the eighteenth century. *The Last of the Mohicans* is pure adventure, dating back to the French and Indian Wars.

Jim Corbett. Hunter and sportsman, Corbett roamed Indian in the early twentieth century, helping villages rid themselves of marauding tigers. His book *Man-Eaters of Kumaon* has been compared to Kipling's *Jungle Books.*

Ben East. A longtime field editor for *Outdoor Life*, Ben East was well known not only for his writing skills, but also for his ability to take stories written by others who were outdoorsmen first, writers second, and transform them into gripping tales.

Billy Ellis. Big-game hunter, esteemed member of Safari Club International and writer of an entertaining memoir in *Hunter to the Dawn* (1988), Billy Ellis is also a Civil War historian. He is a devoted member of the 11th Mississippi Memorial Committee; one of his relatives was among the few from the regiment who survived Gettysburg.

William Faulkner. His works are the South. His story, "The Bear" (1931) is a true classic of American literature.

Jim Fergus. Jim wrote one of the best traveling-hunter books of all time in 1992 with *A Hunter's Road.* His book, *1001 White Women,* is a must-read.

Corey Ford. Perhaps the finest writer ever to appear in the pages of *Field & Stream/ The Road to Tinkhamtown* (1970) can move anyone.

Frank Forester. Forester was the nom de plume of Henry William Herbert, a prolific British writer who moved to the United States in 1830.

William Harnden Foster. His *New England Grouse Shooting* (1947) is still the finest upland bird-hunting book around.

Erle Stanley Gardner. Not only did he write about the outdoors, he also wrote the Perry Mason series.

Jim Hamm. An expert bowyer, he writes about the craft in an understandable, thorough manner, weaving history and humor throughout his descriptions of the nearly lost art of hand making bows and arrows.

Robert Hardy. Robert Hardy is not only one of Britain's finest actors, but also an acknowledged expert on the long-bow and how it is made.

Max Hastings. Max Hastings is helping in the unending battle of Britain between sportsmen and nonsportsmen. He has written extensively about the British Labour Party's efforts to ban fox hunting and other blood sports.

Ernest Hemingway. Where it all begins, and ends.

Gene Hill. Readers used to look forward to each issue of *Sports Afield* just so they could read his "Tailfeathers" column. When he moved to *Field & Stream* in the late 1970s, many followed.

Ray P. Holland. Ray P. Holland wrote two popular books in the 1940s: *Shotgunning in the Uplands* and *Shotgunning in the Lowlands*. Both were notable for their entertainment as well as educational values.

Robert F. Jones. His book *Bloodsport* (1974) has become a cult novel for outdoorsmen.

Elmer Keith. The quintessential proponent of large-caliber firearms. When faced with detractors, his classic response was, "What, you mean I'll kill it too dead?"

Tom Kelly. Tom Kelly is the author of two highly successful and now classic books, *The Tenth Legion* and *Dealer's Choice*. He lives in Spanish Fort, Alabama.

Ted Kerasote. Jay was his editor at *Sports Afield* for twenty years. They have gone through good and bad times, and will always be friends.

Rudyard Kipling. "Rikki-tikki-tavi," in *The Jungle Books* (1894), will always remind Jay of his father. Being exposed to Kipling at a young age no doubt affected the course of his life.

Lawrence R. Koller. His *Shots at Whitetails* (1948) is our favorite whitetail book of all time. Jay's hunting club in the Catskills is maybe a mile through the woods from Koller's old Eden Falls Club, which still exists (although the old clubhouse is gone, replaced by a modern one).

Aldo Leopold. His *A Sand County Almanac* (1949) remains as relevant to conversation today as it was fifty years ago.

Jack London. London wrote an incredible fifty-one books in his lifetime. For an outdoor adventure, his *Call of the Wild* is tough to beat.

Gordon MacQuarrie. Set in northern Wisconsin, his *Stories of the Old Duck Hunters* are humorous, entertaining, and timeless.

John Madson. John Madson wrote for numerous publications, including *Smithsonian* and *Audubon*; his most popular book, *The Tall Grass Prarie*, came out in 1982.

David Mamet. One of America's foremost playwrights would just as soon go deer hunting.

Cormac McDonell. Currently the editor of *Men's Journal*, we worked with him for three years at *Sports Afield*.

Thomas McGuane. A dedicated conservationist, screenwriter, novelist, and essayist, his *An Outside Chance* (1990) is one of our favorite books.

Thomas McIntyre. Thomas McIntyre, one of *Field & Stream*'s hunting editors, lives in Sheridan, Wyoming, with his wife and son. Part of his heart will always be in Africa. Tom has hunted turkeys with both of us near Peter's home in Warwick, New York.

John Miller. Miller wandered through Vermont during deer season, dropping by various deer camps, trying to find out what makes them tick. What he found, with words and camera, was an institution based on camaraderie, common bonds, and family heritage.

John Myers Myers. A friend of Jay's, Andy Dyess, lent him *The Wild Yazoo* and suggested he read it. The country described is in many ways unchanged since the book's publication in 1947. Jay has hunted there a number of times.

Richard K. Nelson. One of the best-known deer researchers today, his book *Finding Common Ground* (1996) has been critically acclaimed.

Ted Nugent. A rock 'n' roller known as the Motor City Madman, Nugent's love for the outdoors is passionate, his attempts to instill outdoor values in today's youth unending.

Dan O'Brian. Author of four novels, a collection of short stories, and *The Rites of Autumn*, O'Brian lives with his wife, Kris, in the Black Hills of South Dakota. *Equinox* is his sixth book.

Jack O'Connor. The longtime guns editor of *Outdoor Life*, O'Connor's theories on using lighter calibers are still debated today.

Sigurd Olson. One of the first and finest naturalists and environmentalists, Olson devoted much of his life to protecting the Boundary Waters Canoe Area in Minnesota. Much of his earlier writing was of hunting. He passed away in 1982, at age eighty-three.

José Ortega y Gasset. His *Meditations on Hunting* (1942) embodies all that true hunters believe.

John Ozoga. A well-known wildlife research biologist living in Munising, Michigan, Ozoga has written extensively about whitetails and the animals that pretty on them.

Dr. Saxon Pope. When he wrote *Hunting with the Bow and Arrow* (1923), he dedicated it to "Robin Hood, A Spirit That At Some Time Dwells in the Heart of Every Youth."

Jim Posewitz. His book, *Beyond Fair Chase*, done in cooperation with Orion—The Hunters Institute, set out ethical guidelines for all hunters, and for the first time truly explored the importance and meaning of the hunting experience. A must-read for all hunters, no matter what their quarry or weapon.

George Reiger. George Reiger was a conservation editor of *Field & Stream*, and is a frequent contributor to many national and local magazines. His books include the Pulitzer Prize runner-up *Wanderer on My Native Shore*, *The Wings of Down*, *The Wildflower's Quest*, and many others. He probably doesn't remember, but Jay shot his first goose while in a blind with him near Easton, Maryland.

Jimmy Robinson. A longtime field editor of *Sports Afield*, Robinson was present on the first discussions about a national duck stamp in 1932; he helped formulate the concept of Ducks Unlimited.

Theodore Roosevelt. What can be said? Past president of the United States, a founder of the Boone & Crockett Club in 1887, helped establish Yellowstone National Park. Perhaps little known is the fact that once, while hunting in the South, he passed up a shot on a smallish black bear, which other members in his hunting party promptly dubbed the Teddy Bear. The rest is history.

Robert Ruark. His *Horn of the Hunter* was one of the classic African safari books. For a look at the glamorous side of outdoor writing, if such a side exists, read *The Honey Badger*.

Ernest Thompson Seton. One of America's first naturalists, in the late 1800s and early 1900s. His pen-and-ink sketches formed the basis for much wildlife art that followed.

Steve Smith. Steve Smith is a fanatical hunter of waterfowl, ruffed grouse, and woodcock. He lives in Michigan, where he manages to "hide from my employers enough that I can hunt six days." He has written numerous books and magazine articles.

Mark Sullivan. His *Purification Ceremony* (1997) is one of the best outdoor adventure/mystery stories of the decade.

Leo Tolstoy. The amount of hunting literature from Russia proved to be astounding. Tolstoy, is, of course, one of the best.

Ivan Turgenev. An uncanny observer of Russians of every class, Turgenev's huntsmen learn the touching and frequently comic secrets in the complex relationships between peasants and their masters. Folklore and insights into nature abound in his books.

Lamar Underwood. Underwood has edited *Sports Afield* and *Outdoor Life*, and has written numerous magazine articles and books, including the recent Skyhorse books, *1001 Fishing Tips* and *1001 Hunting Tips*. We have both had the pleasure of working with him over the years. At *Outdoor Life*, he introduced Jay to his future wife. He is a longtime friend of Peter and his wife, Katie.

Lord Warwick. Writing about shooting parties in the 1800s, Warwick gives a glimpse into the royal lifestyle of the time. There were a few excesses.

Col. Townsend Whelen. A shooter, hunter, sportsman, and true gentleman, he was at various times on the staff of *The American Rifleman*, *Field & Stream*, and *Outdoor Life*.

Lee Wulff. Innovator, conservationist, explorer, expert fisherman, Lee Wulff was a remarkable man. Jay had the pleasure of spending time with both Lee and his wife, Joan, who runs the Wulff Flyfishing School in Lew Beach, New York.

Ed Zern. Ed Zern was the hugely popular columnist for *Field & Stream* magazine, whose "Exit Laughing" on the last page was long a favorite of that magazine's readers.

Index